Arm Your Child

A Parent's Guide for Raising Happy, Positive Kids

By Wil Dieck

ISBN: 978-0-996307-29-1

Wil Dieck has taught martial arts classes at the San Diego Meade Ave YMCA for the past five years. He is a Master Instructor and has been teaching martial arts for over four decades.

The martial arts are a wonderful method of helping to "Arm Your Child" against challenges all kids face today, challenges such as falling victim to drugs and alcohol, joining gangs or becoming pregnant, or even becoming the victim of bullies can affect every child.

If you are interested in helping your child develop the self-esteem, self-disciple and self-confidence they need to be able to say no to harmful attractions then give the YMCA a call.

Give your child the gift of martial arts. It will help them develop the courage they need to solve problems that arrive in their life on their own. It will Arm Your Child for life!

CONTENTS

INTRODUCTION

MR. MIYAGI: "And why, Daniel-san, must you learn how to fight?"

DANIEL: "So I won't have to fight."

- The Karate Kid

Introduction

No doubt a title like "Arm Your Child" raises more than just a few eyebrows. In these violence-riddled times filled with school shootings and other unthinkable behaviors, you might presume I'm speaking of fighting fire with fire. But nothing could be further from the truth.

As a master martial arts instructor I teach students that our weapons are not guns, knives or sticks. Our weapons are our brains, how we utilize or program them with the positive attributes you'll find in this book.

Perhaps a more appropriate, but less appealing title would be "Empower your Child." Although more PC, that title may not have drawn you to opening up this book today.

The first two decades of the 21st century finds us in an unprecedented era of socioeconomic conditions. With the recent meltdown of the economy and its continuing aftereffects, many parents have had to select economic survival over parenting.

Often, the family unit fragments, and a parent finds himself/herself charged with the burden of raising a child single-handedly. Even in the most stable families, quite often the cost of living is now at a point where both parents work from necessity. The responsibility of supporting the family financially can severely shrink the amount of time available for your children, time that previous generations took for granted.

We are also in an era of unprecedented technology in terms of entertainment. Children grow up exposed to fantasy violence through television, movies, the internet, videogames, etc. Most of these shows and, particularly the games, are combat oriented and, alas, the greater the gore, the greater the sales. As a result we find children who feel neglected and powerless, resorting to fantasy outlets where they are made to feel powerful by blowing enemies to pieces or destroying whole planets with advanced nuclear technology.

I'm not saying there's anything necessarily wrong with such entertainment, and I'm certainly not going to take the easy way out and blame entertainment industry for all of society's ills. This entertainment is part of our free market system and this violent entertainment exists because there is a demand for it. I would argue that this demand exists because people, especially our children, use it to try to fill their feelings of powerlessness.

On the other hand, the empowered (i.e., "armed") child is well-adjusted enough to play a violent videogame and realize that its pure fantasy then put it aside. Such a child doesn't act out as a result of their anger and frustration. The goal of this book is to help you empower your child this way.

Our society has long looked upon our children as our most valuable resource. While that's an old cliché, old clichés last a long time because they hit a nerve. We believe them to be true.

I believe that as a society one of our primary objectives is shaping the citizens of tomorrow. I also believe that traditional martial arts classes are an extremely effective method for doing this.

I recommend martial arts training as a method of building character. My recommendation would be to search out the schools in your area that offer these types of programs.

Even if you or your child never puts on a Gi or Dobak (martial arts uniform), the values and character- building process that you'll find in traditional martial arts training can be very effective. The simplest (and stereotypical) example of martial arts training comes by way of the classic story:

Joey gets beaten up by the school bully. Joey's mother enrolls him in a karate class. Joey's mother's motivation is to keep her son from being injured or even killed through self-defense expertise.

However, unfortunately, and typically, Joey's motives are not so pure. Joey wants revenge. He's been humiliated; the class thinks he's a "wimp," the girls look down on him. So he's going to learn karate, go back and punish the bully, and win back his standing at school. Indeed, if another avenue had been chosen, such as a summer of weightlifting and boxing at the local gym, Joey would probably turn into a bully himself.

Joey gets a rude awakening in karate class. First, he has to wear a white belt, signifying that he's the lowest person on the totem pole. He sees there are other white belts in the class, and they don't have a problem with it, so he accepts his status. He also sees advanced color belts and even awesome black belts putting on amazing displays of power. "Just wait, you bully," thinks Joey. "Soon I'll be just like them and then you'll be the ones who have to watch out!"

Joey's next rude awakening. All he's learned is maybe how to do one aspect of a punch, and he's not even that good at it. His instructor says, "be patient, it takes time."

Months go by and Joey still can't defend himself. He's very frustrated, but his instructors and the senior students remind him that everyone starts as a beginner. Bruce Lee and Chuck Norris both had to start at the beginning.

More months go by. Joey gets better. Soon he feels he would stand an even chance against the bully, but instead of fighting him, he finds himself ignoring his taunts.

Joey's mother likes that he's begun hanging around with a better crowd. His grades are improving. At the parent teacher conference his teacher tells his mother how much Joey's concentration has improved.

Joey tests for higher belts. He puts in a lot of practice. He gets promoted. And when he realizes that he could easily defeat the bully in a one-on-one confrontation, he also realizes something else: He doesn't care!

He knows he's good. He's proven it to himself and others. He no longer feels that he has anything to prove it to anyone, particularly another student whom, he realizes is so insecure he has to prove his worth by physically assaulting those smaller and weaker than himself. Rather than seeking vengeance on the bully who hit him mercilessly a few months earlier, Joey now finds himself pitying his tormentor.

Of course, this is just one example of one of the benefits of martial arts training. But it illustrates the objective of this book: To arm your child with the positive attributes and the character that are found in the principles of traditional martial arts training.

With this in mind, let us proceed to arm your child with twelve all-important "weapons," or attributes. Each of the following twelve chapters deals in detail with one of these twelve weapons, and how you can arm your child for not for survival but success in today's world.

CHAPTER 1

Self-Esteem

"What we achieve inwardly will change outer reality."
– Plutarch

The first attribute we'll talk about is self-esteem. Nearly every school of human behavior agrees on one thing: positive self-esteem is fundamental for success in life. As parents, we know how important positive self-esteem is for everyone, especially our children.

How often have you observed a child who is not particularly gifted or athletically inclined excel because he or she had the confidence to try, without letting his or her perceived deficiencies get in the way? They succeed because their self-worth was such that they felt worthy of that level of achievement.

By the same token, how many "gifted" children have you seen that only had a mediocre level of achievement? Their lack of success resulted because the child's self-esteem was low, and they felt unworthy of the achievement.

High performance human beings are able to achieve at high levels because of the way they feel about themselves. They have high levels of self-esteem.

What is Healthy Self Esteem?

"There is overwhelming evidence that the higher the level of self-esteem, the more likely one will be to treat others with respect, kindness, and generosity."

- Nathaniel Branden

Self-esteem is how we feel about ourselves. It's a state of mind. If we looked at self- esteem on the line graph, we would see how it could be positive or negative. People who have healthy levels of self-esteem know that they are lovable and capable. They care about themselves and other people. Healthy self-esteem cultivates a positive, "I can" attitude toward life.

Poor Self-Esteem

"Low self-esteem is like driving through life with your hand-break on."

- Maxwell Maltz

Poor self-esteem is a barrier to high performance. For example, a girl struggles with math because she believes she "isn't any good at math". A boy never tries out for any sports because he is "weak and clumsy". Poor self-esteem tells a child "you aren't good enough" so they give up, often without a struggle.

Most negative behavior is rooted in poor self-esteem. A boy becomes a bully not because he feels superior but because his low self-image fills him with anger. Craving love and acceptance a teenage girl allows herself to be easily seduced. Needing to fit in, children experiment with drugs to impress their peer group.

At the very least, when a child doesn't feel good about themselves it will bring continuous strife between them and their parents. At its worst, poor self-esteem can be seen in drug abuse and self-mutilation. It can even lead to suicide.

What Can A Parent Do?

Helping your child grow up with strong character and self-esteem is one of the most important tasks you face as a parent. You want to know you are doing everything in your power to keep your children away from the effects of the negative social elements they'll encounter. The best way you can do this is to help them build up their positive self-esteem.

What's key to remember is you as a parent can and do make a difference! You can help your children develop a positive image by regularly helping them with their own personal development programs.

Fundamental Sources of Self-Esteem

Healthy self-esteem has four fundamental sources. The first is the knowledge deep down inside that one is lovable. This knowledge is derived from our primary caretakers, our parents and other parental figures. Psychologists have labeled this unconditional love.

Your children need to know that you truly accept them just as they are. You put no conditions on your love. You do this by communicating that he or she is worthwhile just because he or she is alive.

Let them know that they are the only one just like them in the whole universe. In the history of the world no one ever had the exact same DNA as them. (For you biology majors, in 2008, an article in the

American Journal of Human Genetics pointed out this is true, even for identical twins).

Teach your child to celebrate their uniqueness. The bottom line is this, there's only one you and there's only one me. Let your children know that you love them for their uniqueness.

The second basic source of self-esteem is the feeling of competence. It takes more than merely telling your child that he or she is loved to create positive feelings and self-esteem. Your child needs to find it through their accomplishment. This gives them verifiable, solid evidence.

By performing tasks successfully, your child learns that he or she is able to handle his/her environment. By accomplishing these tasks, your child adds value to his/her life, and learns that he/she has something to offer the world.

There are many methods that this can be accomplished. For example, your child can learn competence through academic or artistic achievement, through learning and education, by playing sports, learning a musical instrument, though dance, or taking martial arts lessons, just to name a few avenues.

I must admit I am prejudiced and, as a martial arts instructor I will frequently be using martial arts training as an analogy. This is a result of what I've observed in over 30 years of teaching martial arts and how training in the martial arts can help arm your child with the attributes of success.

For example, in martial arts training a child receives consistent feedback in the form of belt rankings. The various belt colors are visible signs of competence and achievement. When a student passes a test and earns a higher belt level, the student gains a sense of positive accomplishment. They usually receive a belt certificate as a testament to their competence. Other testaments to competence are things such as trophies, certificates, educational awards, etc.

The sense that they are a good person is the third source of your child's self-esteem. Your child learns this through their community's value system. By having a clear sense of the ethical standards they should follow, you child develops a sense of social responsibility. It is much easier for your child to look upon him/herself in a positive way when they have a model to follow.

The fourth and final source of self-esteem is the feeling of personal empowerment. This doesn't mean the child believes that he or she has the right to control other people. It means that the child feels that he or she has ways to control his/her environment. For example, when a child is given a choice between two activities, instead of being forced into the activity someone else chooses for them, they feel they have some control over their environment.

This doesn't mean removing limitations rules and boundaries. Learning to control one's environment within established boundaries is a good way to show a child that he/she does exert influence over the environment and helps to bolster positive self-esteem (go back to the third source of positive self-esteem).

Self-Esteem is Not Arrogance

It's important to note that self-esteem is not conceit or arrogance. These are cries for help and are attempts at hiding poor self-esteem.

Positive self-esteem is your child's inner comfort about being who he/she is. When your child knows he/she's a valuable human being, he or she has no reason to become a loudmouth braggart or bully.

It's only a person with a challenged ego that must constantly point out the deficiencies in others. They do this with the hopes that they can prove that others are just as deficient as he/she feels.

A person with positive levels of self-esteem is not threatened by the strengths of others and is not afraid to recognize the value of others. This is because he/she is aware of and comfortable with his or her own strengths and value.

Parents: Reflections of Self-Worth and Respected Role Models

"I learned the way a monkey learns -- by watching its parents."
- Queen Elizabeth II

You Don't Have to be Perfect – You Just Have to be Available

Stanley Coopersmith, a widely respected psychologist who wrote "The Antecedents of Self-Esteem" concluded in his psychological study of children that healthy self-esteem is "...not related to family wealth, education, geographical living areas, social class, father's occupation, or always having mother at home."

Coopersmith determined that healthy self- respect comes from the quality of the relationship that exists between the child and those who play a significant role in the child's life. In other words, how much your child feels loved by you is one of the most important factors relating to their positive sense of self-worth.

It's important to note that it's not how much you actually love your child, for most parents this is a given. It's how much your child feels loved by you.

All children are born with the potential to like themselves. Your child builds his/her image of him/herself from the words, body language, attitudes and judgments of others.

The responses a child receives from others, especially parents and family, about him/herself determines how he/she views his or her own self-worth in comparison with others. A child's high level of self-esteem is a result of continual positive experiences with the family and other important people in the child's life.

There are several things that parents can do to nurture a healthy sense of self-respect within the child. One of the best things parents can do is to feel good about themselves personally.

How can we teach our children high self-esteem if we don't think much of ourselves? Your children will pick up on subtle messages about their own self-worth from your body language and the way you talk about yourself. As you do to yourself, so you do to your child!

Being openly self-critical in front of your child is to teach your child to be self-critical. For example, if you make a mistake, instead of saying, "I messed up" use a positive response like, "Well, that didn't work. I'll just have to try something else."

If you do feel a lack of self-worth you can do something about it. Take classes at the local community college, find a job that better fits your personality, talk to a friend or start taking martial arts classes. You can even go to a professional counselor. Do whatever you need to do to help you feel better about yourself!

By feeling better about yourself and increasing your own self-worth, you increase the self-worth of your child. The better you feel about yourself and the higher your own level of self-acceptance, the better your child will feel about you, and, therefore, him/herself.

Single Parent Pointers

While many functional, productive children are the products of single-parent households, single parents face an added responsibility in that, quite often, they are seeking companionship and/or remarriage. This is not to suggest that single parents are out socializing at the expense of parenting. However, single parents are faced with a dilemma: If a parent chooses to forego a social life in favor of exclusively parenting, often the child will feel, "Mom or dad is sacrificing for me," and come to believe he or she is in the way of your happiness.

At the same time, a child may resent a new relationship in a single-parents life. The child may feel that the new partner is trying to be a substitute for the estranged parent.

This puts an extra burden on the shoulders of single parents. They have the added responsibility of choosing someone who can be a good role model, one that can help build your child's self- esteem!

Children learn much more by observation than words. For example, if a single parent enters into a relationship with someone who is openly disrespectful to the child or the parent, the child will feel unworthy of respect.

If the person you are in relationship doesn't accept your rules, such as pounding on the door in the middle of night, and your child understands you're your rule is "Don't call after 10:00 P.M.," your child will see how easily boundaries can be broken and feel that they have no meaning.

The point is when you have children you have a bigger responsibility about the types of people you let into your life, so screen potential relationships carefully.

Another problem often encountered by single parents is when to introduce a new partner to the child. Quite often, a parent does not want the child to bond with a new partner because, if the relationship doesn't work out, the child loses that bond. This can leave the child feeling empty and alone.

However, this can be taken too far. If months go by and the child still hasn't been allowed to bond with the new partner, the child can interpret that to mean the parent doesn't feel that the child is worthy of meeting the new partner.

It takes time to get to know a person. A rule of thumb is in a new relationship, it's a good idea to tread carefully for the first three months.

It's best to explain this to the child, so the child understands if things don't work out it's not because of him/her. During the first three months, a single parent can slowly wean the new partner into a relationship with the child, and see how well the new partner and the child get along.

After all, when you bond with a new partner, your child is part of the package that is you. And, above all, you must be certain that your new partner will ultimately be a good parent and a good role model for your child.

Parents as Psychological Reflections

"Mirrors should reflect a little before throwing back images."
- Jean Cocteau

Have you ever thought of yourself as a mirror or, better stated, a reflection? You are. You are a psychological reflection your child uses to build his or her self-identity. To the young child, parents are accurate reflections of his/her own self-worth.

Children receive a lot of input as to what kind of people they are. Positive signals such as "I love you!" "You're a great kid!" and "I'm glad you're part of our family!" give your child a feeling of self-worth.

On the other hand, messages like "You're so clumsy!" or "Why did you do such a stupid thing?" aren't so positive and can leave your child feeling unworthy. That's why it's important to watch your words.

Children are constantly hanging labels on themselves. When you describe your child as "bad," he/she believes he or she is bad. Remember just as you are not your behaviors, neither are your children.

You probably already understand that there is a tremendous difference between being wrong and having done something wrong. There's also a world of difference between having done something bad and being bad.

As parents it's easy to focus on negative behaviors, criticizing your children when they act up or get out of line. The problem is when you emphasize only the negative behavior, your child will think of him/herself negatively.

This can cause his/her behavior to deteriorate even more. Your child acts out, you criticize more. Your child acts out more, you criticize even more. Eventually their behavior spirals out of control.

To avoid this downward spiral, make sure to notice when your child is behaving the way you want them to behave. Instead of always looking for something to correct become a "good finder," things to comment upon positively.

For example, when they are doing their homework or when they are playing quietly with their friends.

Look for the positive in even the smallest matters. Become a "positive reflector," someone who has developed the habit of building your children, and all people in general, "up" instead of putting them "down." By focusing and commenting on these positive behaviors you will also feel better about you. This, in turn helps to create a family with a high level of self-respect.

Your family unit also has a level of self-esteem and what it means to be part of "our family." By developing a feeling of encouragement and high self-respect within the family, you will experience tangible evidence of greater family love and cohesiveness.

An encouraging family environment gives your family feelings like, "What a great family I belong to!" or "I'm happy to be part of this family." These attitudes are developed by being "good finders" rather than "fault finders."

Realistic Expectations

Remember, kids are not all equal. You need to align your expectations with the level of your child's development at their particular stages of growth, not some unrealistic expectations we received when we were growing up. A good way to know what to expect in a child is to pick up a book on child development and study the different stages of growth a child goes through on their way to adulthood. This allows you to check your expectations against a good benchmark and know you are doing the best job possible for your child's healthy development.

How to Positively Influence Self-Esteem

In the Disney movie Winnie the Pooh, the character Tigger sings the song *"The wonderful things about Tig-gers is...I'm the only one!"* The lesson here is to love and appreciate the uniqueness of your child. Like them for who they are.

Children need to know that they are liked (not loved, which is a totally different emotion) for who they are. The easiest way to show that you like your child is to spend time with him or her.

You're busy, and have different roles that need to be filled in various parts of your life. But no matter how busy you may be, make sure you make time for your child so your child knows you enjoy spending time with him/her.

Tell your child you're aware of his/her unique qualities, and you appreciate them. Spend time together having fun. Play games together, throw the baseball, go to the movies, take martial arts classes, etc.

Let your child get to know you as a person and get to know your child as a person too. If it's appropriate, talk about your feelings, your hopes and goals. This helps your child open up and talk about his/her feelings and aspirations. It also allows them to see themselves as the kind of person who makes a good, interesting friend.

If you have more than one child, it's also important that you spend social time alone with each child. This also delivers a strong message to each of your children that they are individually valued and liked by you.

Loving Your Children Means Spending Regular Time with your Spouse or Partner

By putting your marriage first, you are more likely to become a good parental "team." You will have time to build your life and dreams together, which will help your self-esteem and the self-esteem of your spouse.

It also shows your children that you value each other, a great lesson in life for any child. It gives them a living example of how to build and maintain a stable relationship, a lesson your child will carry into his/her future relationships.

Help your Child Build Competence

For your child to feel good about who they are he/she must think of him/herself as competent. This means they need objective proof.

The only way your child can get the type of feedback they need is to be involved in situations where he/she can be successful. This is where it's critical for you to know your child's level of development. Without this knowledge, your expectations can actually hurt your child's self-esteem. Again I refer you to any good book on child development.

When you put your child into new situations, the child may be reluctant to enter them or actually be afraid. Although this is normal for some children, it can cause your child to become discouraged, even before they start.

This is when you, as a parent, must be strong and not allow your child's fears to keep them from trying. You must give them the opportunity to try. Giving in to these irrational fears can lead to your child developing the feeling that he/she can't do new things very well.

If it's truly a task your child cannot do let them know you are proud of them for trying. Then together search for something else your child would like to try and get them involved in it immediately.

If your child is failing at something that they absolutely have to become competent at, such as reading or math, it is important that you get your child special help. Fortunately today there are many resources you can find to help your child in almost any area they need assistance with.

It's important to frame the special help positively. For example, getting the services of a math tutor can be framed as "to make you as good in math as you are in everything else." Also, make sure that you give your child specific and sincere praise for every small achievement he/she makes in that area.

This technique also works if your child is trying a new activity, such as soccer. Let's say your daughter comes home dejected after soccer practice. Instead of saying, "Well, I'm sure you'll be a good soccer player someday" say something more to the effect of, "I like the way you dribbled the ball today," or "That was great the way you passed the ball to Susie during your last scrimmage!"

This allows your daughter to see the improvements she is making and helps her to see how she will learn any new skill, step by step. This builds a feeling of competence and is a good learning experience for everything that she does because of the greater lesson she'll learn, that all expertise is learned step by step. If you put in the time and effort you can become competent at virtually anything, one step at a time.

Building competence one step at a time is especially true in traditional martial arts training. If you have ever attended a martial arts class or watched a martial arts film you may have seen a martial arts practitioner performing a lengthy, intricate dancelike form. For those of you not familiar with the field, these forms are called "kata" or hyungs.

In martial arts training, a person learns a few movements of a new form in each class they attend, learning a new part at each subsequent class. Eventually they put the whole thing together. The end result is proficient performance of something that looks incredibly difficult to the beginner. This continued path to improvement leads to incredible self-confidence and self-esteem in the martial arts practitioner.

Have a Good System of Boundaries

Discipline, or boundaries, are rules for behavior and how we make and enforce these rules. The purpose of discipline is to help your child get along with others, and to grow up with a sense of consequence. The goal is to help your child become self-disciplined.

Kids need boundaries. It's been found that children raised without boundaries have lower levels of self-esteem and a higher level of problems at school and at home.

A good sense of boundaries, of consistently knowing what's expected of them and the consequences they will receive when not meeting those expectations, gives your child a sense of security. They key word here is consistency. By providing your children with consistent discipline you are also giving them a high level of self-esteem.

You can help your children learn discipline through chores at home, working toward goals in school, and practicing sports, gymnastics, dance and martial arts.

Let Your Child to Make Mistakes and then Take Responsibility for Them

Everyone learns from mistakes. From learning to walk to flying a jet plane, everything you learn is by making mistakes.

It's the old story: When a very successful film producer was being asked by a young film student, "To what do you attribute your success?" the producer replied, without hesitation "Making good decisions."

The student became more excited and asked, "How," he asked, "did you get the ability to make such good decisions?"

The producer's next answer was just as swift as the first. "Experience."

The student became even more excited. Thinking he was onto some magic formula he then asked, "And how did you get this experience?"

The producer hesitated, only for a moment, smiled and replied, "Bad decisions."

Now, this is not to say that you should allow your child to make what are obviously bad decisions, such as taking drugs, revenge, skipping school, etc. We believe that it is your responsibility as a parent to give your child a value system that will prevent him/her from making such costly mistakes. In instances where personal safety or the safety of others is involved, your child should always receive the benefit of your experience.

But in those areas where they can learn through experience, it's important to let your child learn it's okay to make mistakes. Through this process your child will learn that this is how we become better at any task we attempt: we learn from our mistakes.

Let your child know it's all right to make honest mistakes. Since everyone makes mistakes, it's important to remember not to overly criticize the spilling of a glass of milk or the knocking over of a potted plant. These things happen, especially to younger children.

When your child forgets to bring home his/her backpack from a friend's house it doesn't mean he/she's careless or thoughtless, and phrases like, "I spent good money for that and you don't even care!" aren't going to help the situation. Making him/her retrieve the backpack (if possible) and setting a deadline for the return of it will, instead, teach him/her to value possessions, to take responsibility for them, and the consequences of not being responsible. If the backpack cannot be retrieved without driving, and there is nothing critical in it (i.e.; asthma medication), let him/her make arrangements to retrieve it as soon as possible, again teaching him/her how to take responsibility.

If there was homework in the backpack due the next day, it also teaches the consequences of not being responsible. Better a late homework assignment than lost school books.

A note here would be that an exception to this advice would be if the child makes the same mistake over and over again. This is an indication of deliberate behavior.

Examples would be if she repeatedly leaves her backpack at Susie's house so she has an excuse to go back and visit Susie, or if he repeatedly "accidentally" forgets to turn on the alarm clock. In these cases you'll have to come up with strategies designed to help your child overcome these blocks and become more self-disciplined.

Finally, remember that activities are the building blocks of teaching your child to be successful. Two of these, which we repeatedly suggest, are team sports and martial arts.

In martial arts, for example, your child will discover that everyone makes mistakes on their routines until they have practiced enough to become good at them. They learn the value of practice, and that by not giving up they can achieve their goals, in spite of their mistakes.

Attention

Every child needs focused attention, genuine communication, and to feel loved. An important way we can show that we value our children, or anyone else's, is to listen to them. By listening to your children and giving them your full attention, you are telling them that you value them and what they have to say. This sends your child the message "You are important to me."

According to Lynda Field in her book, "Creating Self-Esteem," the verb "to listen," in Chinese, is composed of five characters: ear, yourself, eyes, undivided attention, and heart. From this translation she suggests that listening is more than just hearing, but it is the undivided attention of our whole being.

You see, love is always communicated through this kind of intense listening. We won't always communicate love by physical affection, time or gifts. We will always communicate love, really touching someone, by really listening to them. It gives your child or anyone else the feeling "I am valued." We feel valued because someone is trying to understand us at the deepest possible level.

Here are two good rules of thumb to remember when talking to your child about difficult occasions in their lives: One, try to help them identify what it is they are feeling, and two, help your child realize that it was the event that caused the feeling.

An example of this might be when your child comes home from karate practice saying something like, "I'm never going to learn the next routine my teacher showed me today, but Jonathan already has it down! I'm so stupid!"

Instead of trying to encourage your child with, "Oh, I know you can do it," or "You're not stupid," you can use a little empathy. Instead, try something like, "You're upset about not learning your routine today." Then you can add, "And you're frustrated because Jonathan is learning this routine faster than you."

This shows you are actively listening to what your child is saying and it helps them see what it is he is feeling, and why. This also helps your child see the difficulty for what it is, a manageable event he has some control over. This, of course, builds your child's self-esteem. Active listening works because it helps your child see his life from another perspective. By the way, this also works with your spouse or partner.

Another thing to remember about listening is to be there 100% with your child. Put down your portable electronic devices, turn off the television. This will allow you to be in the "here and now."

When your concern is about the past, the future, work schedules, and other tasks, your child will perceive this as a lack of love.

Make it a habit of truly listening to your child, of being entirely with your child in the moment, in the here and now. See what your child sees, the butterflies, the clouds, hear what your child hears, the wind in the trees.

Allow yourself to remember what it is to marvel at nature and life. Not only will it do wonders for your child and your relationship with your child, it will do wonders for you.

Recognition

It is vitally important that you take an active interest in your child's abilities, talents, skills, and interests. It's also just as important to find occasions to where you can praise your child for those attributes.

This works best when there are other interested parties present, such as grandparents, aunts and uncles, cousins, close friends, neighbors, and so on. A child senses that you wouldn't say things to others if they weren't true; in other words, this validates the praise and tremendously boosts self-esteem.

You can show your interest in your child's accomplishments by displaying work your child has done, such as paintings, drawings, a school paper and such on the refrigerator, on a bedroom door, on a mirror or nightstand. Putting it up where everyone can see it will confirm to your child how proud you are of him/her.

Encouraging Environment

Another way of greatly boosting a child's self-esteem is to encourage your child to give praise to others. This tells him/her that his/her opinions are important and valued. One way of doing this is to have weekly family meetings where each member of the family tells something about another member of the family did that week that he/she appreciated. Teach your children to do this outside of the home as well.

Encourage your child to congratulate others when they accomplish something worthwhile. This will not only make your child well-liked, it will teach your child that others are capable of impressive accomplishments, and prevent your child from becoming envious of others.

If your child has a friend who needs help in school, say in math, teach him to give encouraging comments to his friend, letting his friend know he is competent and can do well on the upcoming test. Encouraging is a great way to build self-esteem, and as beneficial to the one doing the encouraging as it is to the one being encouraged.

Let your Child Help

It's also important to let your children help, be it helping around the home, helping you pick flowers for a sick friend you're going to visit, or helping you to do some painting at your church.

It's also important to get your children involved in charity functions at an early age. This gives them an avenue to make a valuable contribution to the lives of others. It also teaches good moral and altruistic behavior.

Helping others is a major character and self-esteem builder.

Honesty

Finally, the praise you give your child must be honest.

For example, if your child recently did well on a math test, but is usually more in the middle of the grade curve, you can't tell him he's the best math student in the school. He'll see right through this, and this will invalidate the rest of your praise.

Rather, tell him how proud you are of how much he's improved. By the same token, if you tell your child he's a super athlete, and the other children are always riding him for a lackluster performance on the soccer field, from then on he'll see your praise as "just words." Instead, compliment him on his kicking or dribbling skills, or how hard he tried in the game.

Children are incredibly perceptive. In giving your child honest praise, your praise will retain validity.

Everyone is going to be strong in some areas and less capable in others. It is important that your child realize that human beings are limited, but each one has value in spite of those limitations.

If your child is struggling with one or more areas of her life, she can still feel positive about herself in spite of these difficulties. If she knows she excels in other areas, she won't feel so bad about her problem areas.

A good example of this can again be borrowed from martial arts training. A good instructor can effectively teach by rewarding a child with recognition for doing what's expected with a promotion in belt level.

A well-trained instructor will also notice the small improvements and let the child know how much she has improved. An example of this might be, "I like the snap you're getting in your front kick!"

Notice that the instructor didn't say "Your front kick is fantastic!" He told the child that he had seen improvement, and gotten specific by commenting on the increased "snap" in her kick. This is the way we should always recognize improvements: positively and specifically.

A Final Note About Self-Esteem

As parents, you want the best for your children. You want them to grow up to be disciplined, honest, competent, productive and responsible adults.

You want them to be men and women of good character, and successful and happy. You want them to make long-lasting friendships and have activities in which they can feel good about themselves.

You want them to have good values. You want them to recognize their strengths, use their talents, and believe in their abilities to achieve whatever goals they set for themselves.

When a child can take pride in him/herself, and his/her accomplishments, and has a good support system, he/she gains a sense of direction and purpose as well as a sense of confidence. What this child has is good self-esteem.

CHAPTER 2

Self-Discipline

"For the very true beginning of wisdom is discipline, and the core of discipline is love."

- From the Wisdom of Solomon (Proverbs 5:14)

Before we can discuss the ultimate goal of arming your child with self-discipline, we must discuss, in detail, where self-discipline originates: with discipline. By being properly disciplined, we become self-disciplined.

Discipline helps our children make empowering choices for themselves. It helps them learn about life in a safe manner. It gives them guidelines on how to live their lives in ways that will take them where they want to go while understanding and respecting others.

Many people see discipline as what we will define as "motivation," ways to influence behavior. For us, discipline involves the rules we have for our children's behavior and how we go about forming them.

In this section we will cover discipline, definitions and formation. In the section on motivation, we have already covered various techniques for enforcing behavior.

Discipline has been defined as 1) Training that produces obedience, self-control or a particular skill. 2) Controlled behavior produced by such training. 3) Punishment given to correct a person or enforce obedience.

We believe that our goal as parents is to use discipline to help our children become self- disciplined. A parent's job is to set workable boundaries and acceptable limits for our children so that they can adapt these for themselves.

We need to set these boundaries in such a way that they protect our children, others, our values and ours and others' property, but in a way that is understandable and reasonable for both the parent and the child.

Teaching proper boundaries can be likened to teaching a person to train lions.

There are many ways to train lions. You have decided you would like to learn to train lions.

The first lion trainer you visit says, "Come on in and watch me."

He goes into the lion's ring and has the lion doing tricks in no time at all. The whip is cracking the lion is roaring. It looks easy and, to the trainer, it is.

After a short time the trainer steps out and says to another student, standing next to you, "Here's a whip and a chair. Go to it!"

You watch as the brave new student enters the ring. The teacher enters with him, shows him how to hold the whip and the chair, then the teacher steps out of the ring to watch the neophyte trainer. The new trainer is indeed brave; he cracks the whip, picks up the chair and says, "Up kitty!" You see, he didn't get quite everything by watching the more experienced trainer.

The lion looks at him and roars. The new trainer's hair stands on end as he drops the whip and chair and runs for dear life to get out of the ring.

This is not exactly what he had in mind, nor what you had in mind either. Therefore, you decided to look for another teacher.

The second teacher is much different.

He walks around with his back straight and his shoulders back. His very demeanor tells you that he's in charge.

He gives you lectures on what you should do, points out all the obvious flaws in your style as you practice outside of the ring, and hits you with the whip if you don't do exactly as he says as quickly as he thinks you should.

He belittles you as he corrects you using sarcastic remarks and often hits you and pushes you around. After doing this for a week, you finally get up your courage and ask him when you'll get to go into the ring with the lion.

He bristles and shouts, "Don't question me! I know what's best! I know when you'll be ready to train with the lions!" Then be begins to hit you with the whip all over again.

He doesn't hit hard enough to cut your skin, but hard enough to hurt. He reminds you over and over again that he's in charge here, and makes you feel small and insignificant. You go home that night realizing that you better find another school, or give up on the idea of training lions.

The next day you are telling a friend your experiences, and she tells you that she read about a great lion tamer in the paper, who is accepting students. You grab a newspaper, get the address, and rush down to meet this great lion tamer.

When you get there, she comes up to you and greets you pleasantly. She tells you how much she's looking forward to working with you and making you into an even better lion tamer than she is.

She, like your last teacher, starts you out on exercises outside the ring to get you used to using the whip and chair correctly. She corrects you, but she also tells you what you're doing right and makes you feel as though you're making progress.

She brings you into the ring and has you work with an old and friendly lion at first, as she stands close by to give you advice and encouragement. Once in a while, when you're not paying attention, doing something that can get you or someone else hurt, your teacher reminds you to concentrate and pay attention. She makes you think about what you're doing.

Soon she's watching you from outside the ring as you and the old lion have a great time doing tricks and roaring. A few weeks pass by and now you're working with more aggressive lions, ones who need more handling. Every time you go in with a new lion your mentor is there, helping you by giving you advice and encouragement, telling you "I know you can do it!" She's also always there to keep you on track, to keep your mind on what you're doing.

Soon you have graduated and you're a lion tamer in your own circus. You're grateful to your mentor for all she did for you but, even more importantly, you have the confidence that you can tame lions all on your own. You know how to take lions without getting yourself or anyone else hurt.

Does this mean that I think children need to be trained like lions, or that teaching children discipline can be compared with lion training?

Well (I had to think about this answer for a minute), of course not. That's really not even the point at all.

The point is your children are going to have to tame many different lions of their own in life. These are the lions of their desires or their appetites.

They'll have to learn to make decisions on their own. They'll need to learn to be responsible. A good portion of what they'll learn is from the boundaries you help them set as children.

They too can learn to be great lion tamers with the proper nurturing and discipline. What you need to do is be the great teacher who handles your children with nurturing and care.

Before we get into a discussion of how to form your boundaries, let's look at the various types of discipline and their effects on children.

Types of Discipline

Essentially, there are four types of discipline:

1. Authoritarian discipline.
2. Over-permissive discipline.
3. Family discipline.
4. Self-discipline.

Over permissive discipline, which was often advocated by certain factions of psychology and psychiatry, is over permissiveness. This is, literally, abdication of the power of the parent to the child.

A common term for this is the "child-centered home." The problem with the child- centered home is that the child doesn't have the resources, judgment or experience to make all of his or her decisions.

Over permissiveness is like the lion tamer who let the student go into the cage with very little training. He'll soon retreat, mentally scarred from the incident, or, worse yet, wind up as the main course of the lion's next meal.

This is because he never learned how to take care of himself in the lion ring. Without proper training and proper boundaries, the child isn't safe from himself or many of the ugly influences of the world.

Over permissiveness was, in theory, a better way to raise children. It was a knee-jerk reaction to authoritarian discipline.

The generation of baby boomers, especially in America, were subject to a lot of arbitrary exercises of authority for its own sake in the schools, such as dress codes, hall passes, and "because I said so, that's why" rules.

As a result of this, this generation tended to swing the pendulum the other way when they had children of their own.

The theory was that a child raised without restrictions would grow up without all the problems seen created by authoritarian discipline. Like socialism, it worked fine on paper.

Like socialism, history has proven it to be impractical in reality. The problem is that it develops children who are even more troubled than children from authoritarian backgrounds. Without the proper training of the lion trainer, the lions are in charge.

Pick up any newspaper to see what over permissiveness did to succeeding generations. Teen- aged pregnancy, gangs, drug abuse venereal disease and people nearing 30, living at home who haven't yet decided what they want to be "when they grow up" are rampant lions in today's society.

It was once remarked that 20 years ago, you could go a fast food outlet for a demonstration of the true meaning of the term "fast food." If there were too many customers in one line, the manager would instantly open another. Five people ahead of you were no problem, you'd be out the door with a hot meal in the bag in a few minutes.

Now, it is not uncommon to have a number of people in front of you and only one line open while the rest of the employees are standing around talking. The cashier seems to invariably be incapable of figuring out which button to press on computerized equipment designed to make the job easier.

Your order is filled with the speed of individuals who move as if they were under water, and if there are more than two people ahead of you in line, be prepared for a long wait.

And surely most readers will have had the unpleasant experience of a worker who first avoids eye contact, then slowly notices you, and either finishes a conversation before helping you or walks over with a calculated indifference, all to make the statement: "I don't have to hustle for you."

I don't bring this example up to stereotype fast food workers, and I apologize to the many fine fast food workers across the nation who really do hustle and care about their customers.

I only use this as an experience probably every reader has had, to point out the stark contrast from one generation to the next. The reason is that we are now seeing the consequences of a couple of generations raised with over permissiveness and no sense of responsibility or sense of consequence for wrong actions or poor performance.

A deep-seated problem with over permissiveness is that by giving up the parental power you rightfully have as a parent ultimately leads to rejection of you and your values by your children. The child in an over-permissive household sees his parents as weak, or even worse, not caring about what happens to him or her.

I have heard this from teenagers I've worked with over and over, "My parents just don't give a (expletive of choice) about me. They just let me do whatever I want."

The child is frightened to be his or her own person because they have no guidance or direction. These children fall prey to outside influences that do not take the child's best interest to heart.

When a child is raised with over permissiveness, it is interpreted as a loud and clear message: "I don't care about you."

The worker who makes you wait intentionally does so because he's desperately trying to send the message, "I'm just as important as you are" because he doesn't feel important.

A child who tries drugs due to peer group pressure does so because he feels (and wrongly so) that his peer group cares about him, so he must conform to their habits. Every child needs concerned guidance from his parents.

Authoritarian discipline is the other side of the coin, when the parents make all of the decisions. They make the rules, give direction in how to follow the rules, and exact punishment for non-compliance to the rules.

This is like the lion tamer who micro-managed. You have to do everything the lion tamer says and you have to do it now!

We're sure you've encountered this type of parent. They're the ones you hear telling their kids "You eat all the food on your plate and you do it now."

When the child replies with something like, "But daddy, I don't like peas," daddy replies with, "I don't care what you like. You do what I tell you to do. You eat all of your food including your peas right now!"

And, of course, there's the battle cry of the authoritarian parent: "Because I said so, that's why!"

In this type of relationship, the parent keeps all the power. The parent is in total control. It is enforced through power.

The parent can give and take away privileges and resources. The parent can give bribes and praise. The parent can arbitrarily change the rules at any time.

Additionally, the parent is, until about the middle of adolescence, capable of physically enforcing any order. All decisions are made for the child and the child has no input.

The Baby Boom generation was subject to a lot of authoritarian discipline. Children during the 1950's and 1960's were frequently told "You have no rights until you're an adult" or "What you think is irrelevant."

Protests or hesitation was immediately met with punishment, sometimes physical. As a result, members of the generation that said "Don't trust anybody over 30" really didn't start to become functional until they were over 30.

"Question authority" was a frequently heard slogan of the day. And, the developmentally stifled generation, as we have seen, swung the pendulum too hard the other way by becoming over permissive parents.

Although we believe that it is very important for parents to give their children direction, for healthy growth, children must be allowed to make decisions for him or herself. They must be given direction, but then allowed to be a part of the process of learning to train the lion, not merely standing outside the ring.

When the lion tamer belittled the student, it was because he wanted the student to know who was in control. When he hit the student for making mistakes, again it was because he wanted the student to know who was in control.

He didn't allow the student to actually go into the ring because he either would not or could not teach the students how to tame the lions very well. He didn't want new lion tamers, he just wanted students who would do whatever he told them. The problem was that students could never become lion tamers without a teacher.

That's the problem with authoritarian discipline: It encourages dependency. There is no incentive for the child to think for himself; indeed, quite the opposite as independent thought is discouraged.

It tells the child, "There is no way for you to tame lions. It's too dangerous. You need our experience to do it for you." As a result the child never learns to set boundaries.

There is an added negative effect that comes with dependency: It creates hostility. The child is only as good as the presence of the authority figure.

A well-known psychological principle, as well as a principle known by all conquerors is that behavior controlled from an outside source is only as good as the presence of that outside source. A nation that has been conquered always needs soldiers and weapons to keep the conquered people "in line."

With children, I'm sure every reader has seen the example of the "perfect child" who runs wild when his parents aren't around.

I'll never forget a personal experience teaching martial arts, when several children from a local private school were dropped off for lessons by one of the mothers. They would always run to the store across the parking lot and load up on candy, which they would guzzle outside the studio before the lesson.

I often wondered what their dental bills must be like, and what that huge amount of sugar must be doing to their systems. Then, one day, one of the kids had a little extra candy and offered it to me.

"Why don't you take it home to your little brother?" I suggested. He responded, "Oh, I have to get rid of it now. I'm not allowed to have candy."

As children raised in an authoritarian environment grow older and starts to find that the limits and rules cannot be as strictly enforced, they start to act out of this repressed anger.

Smoking is a good example: adults smoke, children aren't allowed to, so smoking at an early age is an attempt to enter the world of the "all-powerful adult."

Such children frequently act out in school, run with the "wrong crowd," use drugs and alcohol, become involved in promiscuous sex (another attempt to enter the adult world), or just become terrors in the home. We're sure you would agree that none of these are behaviors you would like to see in your child.

Authoritarian discipline makes a child grow up feeling insignificant. It tears down the fabric of self-esteem.

It teaches children that they are incapable of making their own decisions and discourages them from thinking for themselves. It shows we have no faith in them. It can keep the peace in the short run, but it is highly destructive in the long run.

We want to emphasize that we emphatically believe that there are times when the parent must act as an authoritarian. This is when the child's safety or health is in jeopardy or there is a problem with the law.

This is not repressing the child; this is acting to protect the child. However, the authoritarian discipline under these circumstances must still be very carefully thought through and defined by you in advance so you will respond in a way that will benefit the child.

Family discipline is where the parents share the responsibility of discipline with the children. This is not the abdication of power, and it's not completely democratic.

Parents are in charge of the discipline and it is understood that parents have the power, but voluntarily allow the children a measure of the power to teach them responsibility. This teaches acceptable behavior through shared power and, therefore, shared responsibility.

The lion tamer who taught the student how to be a lion tamer did so through student involvement. She helped the student learn what he needed to learn and reminded him, when he needed reminding, of how important it was to stay within the rules, the boundaries of good lion taming.

Although she let the student learn, and solicited his input, she was in charge because she had the experience and the knowledge, but she empowered him through experience.

Psychologist Stanley Coopersmith points out that every social group, no matter how small, must establish patterns of authority. There must be a delegation of power, status and responsibility to members of the group for the group to function effectively.

An example of this can be seen in driving. If you and every other driver had absolute power to drive down the street, you could, of course, drive on whatever side of the road you felt like driving on. You probably wouldn't make it to a ripe old age because another driver could easily take it in mind to drive in the other direction in the same lane that day.

Therefore, for starters, to be able to drive safely down the road, you give up half of your power and can only drive on one side of the street. Additionally, you must drive at safe speeds, and intersections must be controlled by signals or signs.

If you follow the rules you are free to make your own decisions as to when to drive and where you're going. If you break the rules, law enforcement agencies and the courts have the power to punish you.

In a family organization, parents possess more resources, experience and skill levels than the children. This will remain true at least until the children reach late adolescent years.

The idea of a totally democratic family (one person one vote) is based on the theory that children can make decisions as well as parents. This may, again, work in theory, but, as Dr. Coopersmith points out, "Parents are ultimately responsible for the conduct of their children."

Shared power gives the child input. It empowers them to think, to become responsible for their behavior. This is done through family meetings or gatherings.

The family meeting can be used to set family rules and for bringing concerns to the table. It can be used to share good news and bad news, as well as to ask for help. The purpose of the family meeting is to connect with one another once a week in a truly meaningful way.

Since our society is moving so fast, it's not always possible for everyone to have meals together regularly. This doesn't mean that you can't schedule family time together. This is vitally important for your children's healthy growth. We'll discuss family meetings in more depth later.

The point of family meetings is that research consistently demonstrates the importance of explaining to children the reasons behind family rules and discipline. Parents who give clear, understandable reasons for their actions are more likely to have children who obey the rules, have high self-esteem and behave in a responsible manner.

By explaining the reasoning behind rules parents let their children know that there is logic and love behind those rules. Being involved in the formation of rules will make them more likely to follow them, since they also "own" them.

Through family meetings and the involvement of your children, as your children get older they'll see rules as legitimate and are more likely to follow them on their own. This leads us to the next type of discipline.

Self-discipline, the title of this chapter, is the last type of discipline we'll discuss in these pages. As we stated before, the ultimate goal of all discipline is self-discipline. We want to give our children the ability to make good decisions on their own. We want them to grow into responsible adults.

There is an old proverb that goes like this: "Give a man a fish, feed him for a day. Teach a man to fish, feed him for a lifetime."

To be real parents, we must facilitate our children's growth into maturity; we must teach them how to fish. They must be taught how to discipline themselves. By teaching our children to be self-disciplined we are giving them life skills that will help them with success in many areas of their lives.

When your daughter is self-disciplined, you don't have to lay awake at night wondering if she's going to have sex with her boyfriend at 13. You are confident that she won't because she has set goals for herself and she is disciplining herself to reach those goals.

You're not going to worry when drugs are offered to your son (and they will be offered to your son) if he's going to use them. You know that he won't because he has learned to discipline himself, to curb his appetites.

Incidentally, as a side note, you may have smiled or shaken your head when you read our parenthetical "and they will be offered..." in the last paragraph. Sorry to tell you this: they will be.

Unless a child grows up in an area or under conditions where drug use is almost expected, most parents believed their child would never, under any circumstances, encounter drugs let alone use them.

Statistically, 68% of the illicit drug use among teens takes place in more affluent communities (after all, drugs are expensive). An astonishing 91% of all children have been in contact with or had offered to them some kind of illegal drug before the age of 16.

It's a fact of life: It can happen to your child!

You see, positive self-discipline is making positive choices for ourselves. As your child begins to see self-discipline as a way to achieve goals and dreams, he learns that, as Theodore Roosevelt said, "With self-discipline, all things are possible."

In martial arts training there are constant examples of this process. It is often said that a martial arts student never really learns until he/she starts to teach.

When a student is given the responsibility of teaching a junior belt level class, that student is responsible for teaching the material correctly. Suddenly, the student becomes acutely aware that his form must be perfect or that her technique must be precise. A teacher cannot pass on improper form or technique to students.

I have repeatedly seen students who teach practicing harder than ever and working more diligently than before.

This is because these students, entrusted with the responsibility for turning out students who are, in turn, an extension of themselves, know that they must become role models in the martial arts, and work to become role models. In short, they become self- disciplined martial arts students.

Self-discipline teaches our children to say, "I can reach my goals by putting forth the commitment and the energy necessary to accomplish them." We need to encourage our children to improve the self-discipline in all areas of their lives. In this way they learn to take responsibility for their actions.

We can improve all areas of our lives with increased self-discipline.

Since people learn best by observation and repetition, it is, by our example, as parents, more than any other method or technique that we teach this value to children. We show our children, and others, who look up to us in the community as role models, that self-discipline is central to success.

By demonstrating your self-discipline and success, you encourage your children to also make the commitment to self-discipline.

By the same token, if your behavior is not self-disciplined, this can have disastrous effects on your children. As we've stated before, possibly the most devastating line in terms of raising a child is, "Do what I say, not what I do."

Self-discipline is the attribute which is, perhaps more than any other, subject to teaching through example.

If you are trying to raise a self-disciplined child and you curse other drivers with your child sitting right next to you, you're not going to get very far. If every little thing sets you off into fits of violent temper, you're going to end up with a child decidedly lacking in self-discipline.

One meaning of discipline is "to teach." We believe that we, as parents, need to teach this truth: "Only through self-discipline can we achieve freedom."

The Importance of Discipline

"Parents can't feel right toward their children in the long run unless they make them behave reasonably, and children can't be very happy unless they are behaving reasonably."

- Benjamin Spock, M.D.

Everyone should learn to control his/her behavior. Everyone should learn to channel his/her feelings and actions in a socially acceptable manner. The problem is that many people never do.

Look at any section of the paper and you'll see examples of people who haven't learned to control their behavior. From the heinous crimes of the front page to the listings of divorces, from the behavior of politicians to the obituaries, you'll see examples of how poor self-discipline can make for a poor quality life.

The front page has a story of a man who shakes his baby to death. This is an obvious example of someone who never learned how to control his behavior.

Look at the listings of divorce. Why so many?

While there are very valid reasons for divorce, such as infidelity or spousal abuse, many of these marriages should never have been consummated in the first place.

The vast majority of failed marriages started out okay, but ended in divorce because the people involved never learned to be self-disciplined in an intimate situation.

The morbidly obese man in the obituary who died of a heart attack at 49 may have drawn the short end of the stick genetically but it was his behavior that killed him at such an early age. He simply never learned the discipline of exercise and proper diet.

Discipline affects every area of your child's life. To live well with others, your child has to learn how to deal with frustrations in a way that takes into consideration the rights of others.

By setting reasonable limits and boundaries on your child's behavior and firmly enforcing them, you are helping your child establish his own inner controls and self-discipline. Discipline, tempered by love, teaches a child how to behave in a way that enables him to survive and thrive in society.

By learning how to behave in a socially acceptable manner he isn't rejected by others. In fact, by learning how to behave in a socially acceptable manner he becomes a role model and leader for the other children to follow.

Suitable discipline helps him develop his own identity and gives him an internalized set of values -- a conscience. Good discipline teaches him the ability to put off the impulses for instant gratification and helps him receive the rewards of delayed gratification.

Discipline will teach your child how to channel non-socially acceptable behaviors into socially acceptable behaviors. As you can see, discipline is most important for your child's healthy upbringing.

What about Spankings?

There is a great danger in using striking or spanking a child as a primary form of punishment. When every misdeed is met with a slap on the butt, the child anticipates it and considers it "normal."

He gets emotionally numb to the act, "Oh well, I do this, I get swatted, that's the way it is." It loses its effectiveness.

The other danger is that you are your child's role model. If you strike your child simply because he annoys you or didn't obey your promptly, your child will see violence as the correct way to treat children who annoy him, or to enforce his will upon other children.

Since you are much larger, he may become frustrated over his powerlessness against you, and take out these frustrations by attacking those smaller than he is. Statistically speaking, the vast majority of bullies were the victims of excessive physical punishment in the home.

The only circumstances under which spankings are effective are when it is clear that you only employ them as an extreme measure, and when your normal mode of correctiveness is using positive alternatives to alter the child's behavior.

In other words spanking should only be used in the rarest circumstance and then never in anger and never in a manner that would cause physical injury to your child.

Other Punishments

Punishments such as time outs and removal of privileges have some merit, again when used in conjunction with positive alternatives. When sister pushes brother down and you've told her a number of times that this is not acceptable behavior, you've asked her how she'd feel if this would happen to her, etc., etc., then a time out might be an appropriate punishment.

Time outs are also excellent when a child is acting out his or her feelings rather loudly.

When a five-year-old is screaming and crying over not being able to watch TV, a swat on the bottom would only make the problem worse.

A more appropriate measure would be to say, "Okay, I know you're not happy because you can't watch TV right now, but crying and screaming isn't very nice, and it's not going to change anything."

If it continues, you can follow up with, "Okay, now you're doing this on purpose, so you'd better go to your room." If she refuses to go to her room, picking her up and carrying her there will not traumatize her for life.

Now comes the hard part. If she continues to cry and scream at the top of her lungs, you have to ignore her.

This isn't easy (and hopefully you don't live in an apartment building). But if you come back, she knows it's a way to get you back up there. You've danced to her tune. You have to let her wear herself out so she knows that you can't be manipulated by her tantrums.

When she calms down a little, then you can return to her room and talk to her about how it's not right to yell just because you can't always have your own way. It's all right to disagree, but screaming and yelling is not the answer. Tell her you don't care to listen to it and it will only lead to her having to be put in time out.

After your discussion you can tell her she's still the best daughter in the world, and then display affection giving her a hug and a kiss.

Will this always stop the bad behavior? No.

Will this confirm that you love her, but certain behaviors are unacceptable and will have certain consequences? Yes.

Again, punishments are courses of last resort. You only use punishments when communication fails.

Your first option is to always communicate your feelings while reminding your child of the rules. If your child exhibits defiant behavior after the communication process, my belief is that as a parent you have the right and duty to apply sanctions.

Creating Discipline

You want to create reasonable boundaries, reasonable discipline, but still protect the child. To do this, use the following steps:

1. Have a structured environment.
2. Make sure that your child understands the rules and why you have set the rules.
3. Make sure your child knows the consequences of not following the rules and stick by those consequences.
4. Reinforce your child positively when he/she follows the rules.
5. Make your goal to help your child become self-disciplined.

Now let's take a look at each of these steps.

Have a Structured Environment

The research of the Harvard preschool project, started in 1965, caused its director, Berton L. White, to comment: "In the homes where children are developing well, as contrasted to the homes where the children are developing poorly, we have always seen mothers running the home with a loving but firm hand. The babies in these home situations rarely have any questions as to who is in final authority."

"In homes where the children are not doing well, however, there is often ambiguity with respect as to the setting of limits and who is going to have the final say in disagreements."

What the Harvard research seems to suggest is that firmness and structure combined with love seems to give children a maximum feeling of security and the best opportunity for healthy personal growth.

When you have a clear daily structure your child will know what's expected of him and when.

For example he'll know "We eat at 6:00 P.M." He'll also know that "Bedtime in our house is at 8:30 P.M."

A structure helps your child to feel secure. They see the world as predictable.

This is important for a child's healthy psychological development. When there is no structure, when the world is unpredictable, the child will begin to develop behavioral problems.

What kind of structure and schedule am I advocating? It depends on how old your child is. Again I would refer you to a good child development book for these age guidelines.

Above all, no matter how old your child is, the first thing to remember is to give plenty of love. Love is the primary ingredient to all discipline.

Let's look at babies; infants.

You cannot love an infant too much.

Babies cry.

That's how they communicate with the outside world. You would never punish a baby for crying, but you would try to discover what caused your baby to cry.

It may be because she's hungry or thirsty. Maybe she needs a diaper change. It could be that she's feeling sick with an earache.

Parents learn to notice which cry is for hunger and which is for the change of the diaper, or when she's not feeling well. Sometimes she'll cry because she's bored.

Whatever it is, as a good parent you should make sure your baby knows she's loved and that her world is predictable. One of the best ways to help your children have a predictable environment is to provide them with the consistency of a schedule.

"We go to bed at 8:30 P.M., so it's time to start picking up your toys."

This gives your child a feeling of security within her environment. Her life is predictable. Predictability gives security.

Set a time to wake up. Have a time for them to eat breakfast, lunch and dinner. Have a certain time for watching T.V. Put them to bed at the same time every night.

By giving them consistency you are giving them security. You are also teaching them discipline, even at a young age.

Structure provides security for your child in other ways. When your child is very small you provide some of this structure by child-proofing your home.

We do this because all humans are curious by nature. It doesn't make sense to leave things out that you don't want your small child to get into, so you put your fine knickknacks away.

You use child-proof hooks on the drawers and doors you don't want your child to get into. You put covers over the electric outlets.

By putting up temporary barriers you keep your child where you want her, and out of where you don't want her. This eliminates much frustration from your life and your child's life before it starts.

If we do this for our children at an early age, doesn't it make sense to keep doing this for children as they grow older?

Why tempt them with alcohol left out in the open, or access to television programs and videos we don't want them to see (at least without us to talk with them about it)? Why leave your child things that could get him into trouble, or worse?

If you are a firearms owner, would you dream of leaving a handgun and ammunition accessible to your child? Of course not!

Just as you keep some things from small children because it's good for them, do the same as your children become older because it's good for them too.

This is not to say that you don't trust them. It's just saying that humans are, by nature, curious and that curiosity can sometimes be dangerous in the immature mind.

Even as they grow older, remember to continue with your schedule. There's a time to go to bed and a time to get up. They eat at scheduled times. They continue to be secure by knowing what is happening in their world is consistent.

Again, be sure that the schedule you set is appropriate for your child's age. 7:30 P.M. may be a good time for an elementary school aged child to be in bed, but it's certainly not appropriate for a teenager.

One point to remember is while it is important to make a schedule, don't become a fanatic about it.

When grandma and grandpa are visiting, and bed time comes around and everyone is talking, playing and having a good time, you don't need to put the kids to bed. Remind everyone that bedtime is usually 8:00 P.M. but because grandma and grandpa are there the kids are getting an extra half hour (or whatever) to visit with them.

This shows them that there are exceptions to the rules and also gives them some warning that there will still be a bedtime, even with this exception. (This will also prepare grandma and grandpa for the kids' departure for bed later on.)

A good way to enforce your schedule in a way that helps your child become more self- disciplined is by announcing the time before the event.

For example, instead of saying "It's 8:00 P.M. Go to bed!" try to help your children by saying, "its quarter to eight, time to clean up and get ready for bed."

If they're still doing something a few minutes later, reiterate by saying, "Okay. It's now five to eight. Put everything away. It's time for bed!"

By giving them some lead time, children are more likely to respond positively to scheduled events.

Another thing you can do, especially at the preschool age, is to provide plenty of distracting or alternative outlets for their energy. Kids at this age have so much energy that it's imperative that they have suitable equipment outside, or somewhere in the house, to play on. They need to exercise the large muscle groups and they need to release all that pent up energy.

Adults call this energy "tension." Whatever you call it, you need to let the little ones get rid of it.

Make Sure that Your Child Understands the Rules and the Why Behind Them

As your child becomes older it becomes more important to teach. They need to learn about not going into the street or what containers they should stay out of.

Remember, the primary reason for discipline is to allow people to get along in society. You need to teach your child how to do that. One of the best ways to teach discipline is through family gatherings or meetings.

Family meetings are just what the name implies: the gathering of the family to discuss things that are important to the family.

These important matters include setting family rules, planning vacations, planning outings, sharing victories and receiving support for challenges in life, as well as giving and receiving praise. The list of matters at a family meeting are only limited by the amount of interaction you want to have with your family.

Let's start with making the family rules.

Family rules are rules for behavior in and out of the house by family members. This includes the consequences of not following the rules.

Remembering that the underlying current behind all discipline is love, the family meeting should be put together in a way that gives the family a positive feeling of togetherness.

When discussing a family rule, such as Johnny cleaning his room, ideas should be brought up and discussed as to why it is so important that he clean his room. This gives Johnny the reasons behind why cleaning his room is important.

You should also come to an agreement as to what the consequences are when the room isn't clean. This way you are communicating to Johnny what you expect and, through discussion, you can call help Johnny know what to expect if the room becomes untidy.

Thought this discussion you teach Johnny about good communication skills. By soliciting Johnny's input he will own part of the decisions for the rules and the consequences. This makes it more likely he will do his best to live up to his end of the bargain.

Let's look at a quick example of keeping Johnny's room clean. He's just learning to keep his things in order. He knows what tidy is and where he should put his things. Now is the time to formalize his room remaining tidy.

MOM: Johnny, you've been doing a good job of picking up your toys. Your father and I think you can be responsible for keeping your room clean.

JOHNNY: Well, okay. What do I need to do?

FATHER: What do you think needs to be done, Johnny?

(NOTE: By asking a question the father is empowering Johnny to think of a solution. More on this later.)

JOHNNY: (After a little thought.) Probably picking up my clothes and putting away my toys.

MOM: What about your bed?

JOHNNY: Yeah, making my bed too.

MOM: What else is involved in keeping the room clean?

Johnny and his parents go on about this until they have some kind of agreement on what a clean room means to all of them. Then they go to the next part, the consequences.

FATHER: Johnny, what should happen if you don't keep your room clean?

JOHNNY: How about no T.V. until the room is clean?

(NOTE: This is a logical consequence, not a punishment. Johnny won't have the privilege of using his time to watch T.V. until he uses his time to clean his room. We'll discuss consequences shortly.)

Through the family meeting you are teaching your child how to discipline themselves. You do this by communicating the why's and how's of discipline with them. Now you are well along the road to helping your child become self-disciplined.

The other reasons for having a family meeting are planning family outings and vacations. This helps to make the family meeting a fun time rather than just some mandatory attendance situation to go over the rules.

Also it sets the family up to what it's supposed to be: a support group for every member. It is a safe place for people to share victories and challenges.

It helps you as parents focus on the positive characteristics of your children, which is very important for every member of the family. When your children are very young it's easy to celebrate every new step they take.

Unfortunately, as your children grow older, your focus can change from each positive step to each negative, or misstep they take. By having a formal time to focus on the positive, it helps you get into the habit of focusing on what you want, and to let your children know what behaviors you value from them. It gives you a time to formally acknowledge what you as a family love about one another.

You can take time to just praise a person in the family who is doing or has done something outstanding. You can celebrate the great report card or getting picked for the team. It may be something as small as learning a new song on the piano.

What's important is that the family be thought of as a support group, a place where we like to be, not this place from which we can't wait to escape. Family meetings can make the atmosphere of the house into an atmosphere of love and support. That's why we recommend them so highly.

Make Sure Your Child Knows the Consequences of Not Following the Rules and Stick by Those Consequences

Once your child has worked out a rule with you at the family meeting, there should also be a discussion of the consequences of not following the rule.

In the preceding example of Johnny not keeping his room clean, let's say Johnny comes home one day from school and starts to watch T.V. You know his room is in disarray because you had to drop off his clean clothes earlier.

The first thing you might do is ask Johnny, "Is your room clean?"

Johnny will, at this time, remember that his room isn't clean and that he's agreed to keep it clean. He's also aware of the consequences: no T.V. until his room is clean.

If he now says, "But Mom, I just want to watch my favorite show!" you can say, "I know that you'd like to see your show, but remember, you agreed to keep your room clean and that the consequences of not keeping it clean was to not watch T.V. until it is clean."

What is important to note is you are stating the rule and the agreed upon consequences. You are not telling him what to do.

Before we go further, let's talk about the term "consequences." What are they?

First, let's tell you what they are not. They are not punishments for "bad" behavior. A punishment is when someone in authority does or causes to have done something to someone who acts incorrectly.

An example of punishment might be a person is caught stealing a lawn mower. They are arrested, go to court, and get sent to jail. An authority figure, the court, puts the person in jail for wrong behavior. This is a punishment.

On the other hand, a natural consequence of someone caught stealing a lawn mower might be to give back what they've stolen, apologize for stealing it, and mowing the person's lawn a number of times to make up for the inconvenience of that person having had to get by without a mower.

Admittedly, this is an extreme example. However, if you get the picture, it's a good example.

You need to allow your children the proper consequences for not following the rules. This works a lot better than trying to punish them for violations.

As mentioned before, the problem with using punishment or force as a way to create discipline means that the person is not disciplined when the authority figure is not present. In other words they are not self-disciplined, which is the goal you want them to achieve.

When we get to the section on motivation we'll talked about external motivation as opposed to internal motivation. For right now, realize that punishment is external motivation; correct action out of the fear of punishment.

Consequences, on the other hand, instill a behavior that is internally motivated. It does this by invoking a basic law of nature: "For every action there is an equal but opposite reaction."

Consequences result from cause and effect. They are a logical outcome to negative behavior.

In the clean room example, we came up with no T.V. as a consequence. Why was this a good "logical" consequence?

It's a good "logical" consequence because the time used for watching T.V. could be used to clean the room if the room wasn't clean. It didn't take away T.V. watching for a week, which would have been punishment. Again, we'll discuss how to create consequences more in the chapter on motivation.

Reinforce Your Child Positively When He Follows the Rules

As stated previously, and it's worth stating again, there is one true rule about human behavior. Reward the behavior you want or you'll get the behavior you reward. In other words, if you want your children to behave in a certain manner notice and reward that behavior.

If you've been having a hard time with your five-year-old listening (and who doesn't?), when she listens and gets ready like you've asked her to, tell her "Thank you so much for listening and getting ready so quickly! I really like it when you listen!"

Notice that you've been specific and sincere. Both are needed for reinforcing good behavior.

If you are not specific and say something like, "What a good girl you are!" your daughter has no idea why she's good or that you noticed what she's done. In fact, until this point, she's probably not even noticed what she's done.

Additionally, you were sincere. If you would have said "You're the best daughter in the whole world because you got ready like that," she'll see right through it. Kids are very perceptive. If the praise is insincere, you'll soon lose credibility with your child.

Remember, when noticing good behavior be specific and sincere.

Make Your Goal to Help Your Child Become Self-Disciplined

> *"Right discipline consists, not in external compulsion, but in the habits of mind which lead spontaneously to desirable rather than undesirable activities."*
>
> **- Bertrand Russell**

Finally, when everything's all said and done, you must make it your goal to help your child become self-disciplined. Self-discipline involves the proper motivation for doing the right things and the responsibility one receives by being able to make those empowering choices.

Self- discipline gives your child the ability to accomplish the goals he or she sets. It also helps them make good decisions such as eating the right foods, exercising regularly, getting to bed on time, reading regularly, helping others and setting and accomplishing goals.

Helping your children become self-disciplined is not the easiest path. It's much easier to be a military parent and order your children around.

This never lasts!

Abdicating all power and allowing your children to run free is also an easy way out, but you'll pay for it in the long run. Only by helping your children to become self-disciplined will you have fulfilled your duty as a parent.

Chapter 3

Focus

"We are not troubled by things, but by the opinion we have of things."

– Epictetus

Race car drivers know something which relates to life in general: The car turns in the direction they're looking.

These drivers travel at such speeds that their driving must be instinctive, and the steering wheel follows their focus. If a race driver wants to pass another car, he has to focus on the gap; the space between the other car and the wall. If he focuses on the other car, he'll turn into the other car.

To pass safely, the trick is to focus on the gap. The driver has to focus on the direction in which he wants to go.

That's how focus works in life. You'll go in the direction you focus your thoughts.

It's how focus works in your children's lives also. The way you think, how you focus your mind, will determine both the direction and distance you help your children's journey in life.

Focus on problems, they'll go toward problems. For example, if your child isn't listening to you, you constantly say to your child, "You're not listening to me!"

Where's your focus? It's on the problem!

The trick is to have a different model; a perhaps new way of looking at the world. You have to teach yourself and your children to focus on the solution, not the problem.

In the illustration where your child isn't listening to you, your objective is to get your child to listen. Do your best to catch your child doing the behavior you want, no matter how rare this is.

Your child listens and cleans up his room. You say, "Thank you for listening and cleaning up your room."

You've focused on the outcome; i.e., the solution, a clean room. You either focus on the behavior you want or you'll get the behavior on which you focus!

Simply put, the human mind works on three fundamentals:

1. The mind can only focus on one activity at a given point in time.

It's no use trying to listen to someone while you're watching television. In reality, you can do one or the other.

Your attention is going to be divided and alternated between the other person and the television (if you are like most people more directed toward the television). This means you miss out on parts of the conversation and the program.

To really listen, you have to look directly at the person and shut out (or, better yet, turn off) the television. This way you can really focus on what is being said.

2. Your mind can't bypass a "don't."

Imagine yourself in a dark room. Someone turns on the light and says "Don't look at my face!" Where does your focus instantly go? To the other person's face!

As I write "Don't think about pink elephants," what image flashes through your mind? A pink elephant of course!

This is because the mind has to see itself doing something before it can tell itself not to do something. It can't simply bypass what you're telling it not to do.

A great example of this was the famous Milwaukee pitcher Warren Span during the World Series. All he had to do was get one more out, the last game would be over, and his team would win the series.

His manager came out to the mound and told him, "Don't pitch it high and outside," then went back to the dugout.

He thought about what his manager told him and pitched. Where do you think the ball went? Right! High and outside! His mind couldn't bypass the "don't."

Lifeguards and crossing guards have found that by saying, "Walk, please!" instead of "Don't run!" children around swimming pools and crossing streets are more likely to instantly stop running and start walking.

As a matter of fact, when you see someone running, if you say "Don't run," even if they obey the command, they will always accelerate slightly before slowing down because the mind has to conform to the "don't" act before it can invoke the "don't" command.

3. We go in the direction of our focus.

When race car drivers are passing, they don't focus on the wall because they don't want to end up a spot on the wall. They don't focus on the other car because they don't want to ride to glory on someone's grille. They focus on the gap between the car and the wall, as previously stated.

The reason race car drivers do this is because they know the car will go where they are focusing and they want to make it through the gap.

If you want your child to listen better, you focus on the good listening and the benefits of listening, not the non-listening. Your child is better than the non-listening behavior, so use your focus to prove it to your child instead of reminding them of the fact that they're not listening. They're going to believe what you do a lot more than what you say.

Every day we have the option of focusing on what's working or what's not working. In theory, we're all trying to fix the problem.

Most parents look at what's not working and try to fix it. The problem is that, instead of fixing the problem, they're fixing the blame. Instead of being solution focused, parents become blame focused.

Johnny comes home with a less than admirable report card for the first time in 7th grade. It gets your attention.

You call Johnny over and say, "Johnny, this is a terrible report card! What's the matter with you? Aren't you studying? Don't you care about getting good grades in school?"

You feel justifiably annoyed at this report card. You know that Johnny can do much better. Why did he get terrible marks?

On and on you go in your mind about the report card. Your focus is on the problem, on attaching blame to Johnny's poor performance.

Now, let's look at a solution-based discussion of the report card.

Johnny comes home with the aforementioned report card. You look at it and he's got your attention.

Your focus then becomes: "What can I do to make Johnny's report card better?" The answer is nothing.

You certainly can't make the present report card better, it's done. It's history. There's a problem but the solution isn't going to be found on this report card.

The truth is, only Johnny can make this report card better. He's the one who has to study. He's the one who has to do the work. Your job is to help him focus on the solution to the problem, not the problem itself.

You sit Johnny down for a talk about his grades. You direct the conversation through questions because you need to understand where Johnny's coming from before you can ever give him any input of your own. Only after finding out where Johnny's focus lies can you help him then redirect that focus.

You then ask Johnny: "Are you satisfied with your marks?"

There's an excellent chance he won't be and he'll tell you so, or he may not. There are an infinite number of possibilities when dealing with any human being.

If you have a good relationship with Johnny, most likely he'll talk to you about it. If not, you might have to ask some other questions and reevaluate your relationship with Johnny.

Nobody ever said parenting would be easy, only that it's the most worthwhile undertaking there is.

Johnny tells you that he was so busy hanging out with his new friends and playing on the basketball team that he really didn't have much time to study or for homework. He adds that he did most of it in study hall and that he and his friends worked together on it, some doing the math, some doing English, but all his homework got turned in.

He also tells you that he looked over all the homework and understood it, so he didn't see anything wrong with what he'd done.

At this point you can either fix blame or fix the problem. You can go into a tirade about how homework is really a set of drills to make you learn the material, you can harp on how unethical this is, and so forth.

But you don't. Why? Because you are focused on the solution, not the problem.

Instead, you ask him questions which will, hopefully, help him focus on what school is all about: learning.

You ask, "Are you still planning on going to college?"

Since you've already spent time with him on this issue, you know the answer will be "Yes."

"You're aware of what it takes to get into a good college?"

Again, you receive an affirmative response.

"Then what do you think you should do to make the kind of grades you need in order to be accepted for college."

At this point, he'll come up with answers, and he'll stick to them because they're his answers. Hopefully, they will be goal oriented because he knows full well what's required.

At that point, you ask, "How can I help you bring these grades back up?" or "Is there anything I can do to help you out?"

Now, at this point, volunteering solutions too early or directing his behavior won't get his long term behavior changed. You let him respond, then write down a plan together that will help Johnny direct his focus toward getting better grades.

You help him track the solution from time to time, but you let Johnny take care of it. Your response hasn't been problem-based, it's been solution-based, and so is Johnny's. You've done this by asking questions about goals he's already set up.

Helping your children focus on goals they want to reach is a very important part of parenting.

Let's say your child wants to learn how to improve in basketball. To help him with this, you need to help your child focus on how to improve rather than on what he's doing wrong.

For example, if your child does not dribble very well with his left hand, you wouldn't say, "Your game isn't very good because you can't dribble with your left hand." This will only make him focus on the fact that he can't dribble with the left.

Instead, you might say "Dribble the ball with your right hand. Very good. Now let's see the left. I notice you're better with your right hand than your left. Why don't we practice dribbling with just the left hand until it's as good as the right?"

You've given him positive reinforcement by pointing out that he's good with his right hand, you've pointed out the need for improvement with the left hand, and you've implanted the goal of making the left hand as good as the right hand. You've also done this in a positive manner by saying, "Until it's as good as the right," which has reassured him that, in your estimation, it soon will be.

Our perception of everything in life depends on our focus. You can help your child control his focus. You can teach your child to focus positively.

A good way of doing this is by asking him questions that help him focus on the positive characteristics of a person, place or event. The trick is to focus on what is working, or what could work, rather than what's not working.

In learning to play basketball, you might ask him, "How can you improve your free throw shot?"

Then you could help him come up with a number of answers to that question and write them down. Your questions help steer your child in the right direction.

The same concept applies to how we help children see their lives. Some questions for living life positively might be: "What did you like best about today?" or "What did you like about that person you just met?" "What do you find most interesting about this?"

These are all positive questions, which will direct the focus in a positive channel.

Now, this is not a "power of positive thinking" pep talk. Although we believe most people don't think positive, and would be better served by thinking positive, we absolutely do not believe in teaching children to hide or repress their true feelings, such as anger, hurt, disappointment, fear or sadness.

These feelings must be brought out and dealt with. To suppress your feelings is to suppress what you are. People who deny what they are become dysfunctional.

A popular put-down of the past decade or so is "He's so negative!" A very self-deceptive phrase of people in a state of suppression is, "I just don't associate with negative people."

Invariably, we find that the "negative" person is simply someone who disagrees with the speaker, and it is actually the speaker who is engaging in negative behavior by judging and condemning another for his personality attributes or point of view.

For example, if one is always saying "Be sure to buckle your seat belt because I don't want you to get killed on the freeway," the statement is negative and dire, but the motivation for saying it is positive.

Yes, it would be better to say, "Don't forget to buckle up. I love you and want to be sure you're safe," but even the negative statement is better than simply not caring.

Modern "new age feel-goodism" has done an entire generation a disservice by stating that by avoiding "negativity" (as if it were some wicked supernatural force) and by "thinking positive" we can have anything we want, as if we have discovered some mental Aladdin's lamp.

As a result, we have produced a generation of young adults who constantly condemn those with opposing viewpoints as "negative" as they grow older and older while waiting for their "positive thoughts" to manifest in a lottery win, lucrative job offer, movie career or "Prince/Princess Charming."

One does not ignore negative circumstances, emotions or feelings to make them go away. In the book "How to Talk So Kids Can Learn at

Home and at School" by Adele Faber and Elaine Mazlisa, Ms. Faber points out that we need to recognize our children's feelings.

She tells of the day her daughter announced, "I hate Grandma!" Faber quickly told her daughter "That's a terrible thing to say! You don't mean that!"

With that, Ms. Faber realized she'd just told her daughter that her feelings didn't matter.

If children are constantly told to deny their feelings they will, and the result will be a dysfunctional family and perhaps a dysfunctional person. Everyone has feelings of anger, sadness, fear and disappointment. These are normal, not bad. Bad feelings are those we don't examine, the ones we hide from ourselves.

Eventually, children will simply tune us out and turn us off when they are not allowed to have feelings of their own. If your daughter feels awful because she was cut from the All-Star team and you say, "Oh, Honey, that wasn't so bad. Some kids don't even get to try out for it," you are telling your daughter that her feelings don't count.

Allow her to be disappointed, angry and sad. You don't have to agree with everything your children feel, but it's of utmost importance that you recognize and respect those feelings.

Once your daughter's feelings have been acknowledged, she can begin to deal with them. You could give your daughter a lot more support simply by saying, "Yes, Honey, I know how bad it feels when you don't get something you've worked so hard for." This acknowledges her feelings and helps her put them into words.

You can also tell her a story from your childhood where something similar happened to you. This way, she realizes that disappointments come to everyone from time to time and, since she can see that you obviously grew up into a productive person, there is life after the All-Star team.

Summary

Focus is the one important attribute and quality where you can help direct your child. It is a basic law of nature that we go where we're focused.

Use these questions to help your child maintain a positive focus:

1. What was the best thing that happened to you today?

2. What did you do today better than you've ever done before?

3. What did you do today that let you know how special you are?

4. Of all the things we do as a family what do you like best?

CHAPTER 4

Responsibility

"Taking responsibility for your behavior, your expenditures and your actions and not forever supposing society must forgive you because it's 'not your fault' is the quality most needed in the next century."

- Barbara Tuchman, two-time Nobel Prize winner

As parents, teachers and role models, we need to provide opportunities for our children to become responsible individuals. This means allowing them opportunities to make their own decisions.

Children need to learn to take on responsibilities, rather than having their parents do everything for them. Children learn confidence by doing, by trying and experimenting.

To feel important and to grow, everyone needs to be allowed to take risks. Risking implies the possibility of making wrong decisions but, as discussed in the last chapter, making the wrong decision can be a beneficial learning experience.

When you allow your children to make decisions, you are communicating to them that you trust their judgment. Of course, judgment is a developmental thing, and a good parent has to make the judgment call of how far to set the framework in which the child must make a decision.

It might be impractical, for example to allow a four year old to choose her clothing; however, it is quite practical to choose two sets of clothing and let her choose between the two sets what she will wear that day.

Ultimately, decision-making capacity will increase, and a child will develop good judgment when this is nurtured. Children who learn early how to make the correct decisions as to with whom to associate, what to wear, what to eat, etc., without endangering themselves, learn very early to feel good about themselves.

How do we teach our children responsibility? Read on.

Types of Responsibility

When talking about responsibility, for what are we asking our children to be responsible?

First and foremost, we are trying to make them be responsible to us for their behavior and actions. Next, they should also be responsible for their possessions and the possessions of others.

Third they need to be responsible for the choices they make and what they do with their time and talents. Finally, they need to be responsible for others in their family and society in general.

Responsibility for Behaviors and Actions

A sad fact of life is that few people take responsibility for their own behavior. Read any newspaper if you don't believe this.

A father who shakes his infant son to death is shown to have been abused by his own father, so the court finds his responsibility is diminished. A man approaches a woman with a knife, threatens her and steals her car, and the court is lenient on him because he grew up in an impoverished area and his father deserted the family when he was two. Therefore, it is felt, society has failed him and he should not be held responsible.

Why is this? Why do people so often look outside of themselves for a responsible party, when we can see that they are obviously avoiding their own responsibility?

It's because people have been conditioned to avoid responsibility. Most people avoid responsibility because they have been taught, since childhood, to believe that accepting responsibility is going to have negative consequences. They've learned that when they admit they make a mistake, they are made to pay for the mistake.

Conditioning Your Child to Accept Responsibility

When a four-year-old spills a glass of milk and receives an angry outburst from their parent such as, "Why can't you hold onto that glass?" he sees himself as inadequate and believes that he has failed his parent.

Since we all get many, many of these messages during our formative years (and some us receive even greater negative input, such as physical punishment) it's no wonder we become gun shy about admitting that we've messed up.

Truthfully, as you read this book, ask yourself if you've ever been in a situation where someone said, "Who did this?" and you didn't admit you did because you were afraid there would be a negative consequence. Then, after all was said and done, you learned that the intention of the person who asked was to commend who did it on what a good job was done.

Going back to our spilled milk example, a healthy reaction is simply, "Hey, things happen. Don't worry, it's not like you're the only person in the world who ever spilled a glass of milk. Come on, you can help me clean it up."

If this happens in public and you scold your child even more loudly than you would in private (because you're angry because everyone's looking in your direction), or give your child a slap or glare, this is even worse. You're teaching him that to make a mistake will lead to open criticism in front of others.

The point is that once the milk is spilled it's going to stay spilled. No anger or lecture will get the milk back into the glass. By criticizing, scolding or belittling your child, you're teaching him to avoid taking responsibility. But the fact remains that the milk has been spilled.

By teaching your child to tell the truth and accept responsibility for what happens, without making him feel bad about it or humiliating him, your child will learn to accept what his actions bring and get on with life. He learns that mistakes are part of life and that, instead of being avoided, they should be examined and turned into learning experiences.

The Absolute Importance of Responsibility

While we leave it to political philosophers and sociologists to sermonize about society's ills, we do believe that one of the main flaws in today's society is a lack of responsibility.

In today's society, people tend to be nearly obsessed with fault finding. There is no longer such a thing as human error or random happenstance. Everything that happens has to be somebody's fault.

Even in the corporate world, when something negative occurs, the boss will often instruct his immediate subordinate to "Find out who's responsible for this!" Unfortunately, it's generally the one at the bottom of the food chain and not necessarily the person who actually created the problem who gets the blame.

The result is a lot of finger pointing and "The fault is with him/her" accusations. When a person really does this, what he's saying is "Hey, world, it's not my fault! I have no responsibility in this matter!"

When the boss is looking for someone to blame, what he's really saying is, "Let's make sure I don't get blamed."

This is because, as you read in the last section, that most people have been conditioned to avoid taking responsibility. However, the assumption of responsibility is a cornerstone of character and leadership. One can only lead others if he or she is willing to assume the responsibility for what happens to those others.

The past generation has seen a dramatic increase in lack of responsibility. A prominent schoolteacher once related her 20 years of teaching experience like this:

"Twenty years ago, we had a very authoritarian mentality on the part of the parents. We were almost reluctant to punish a child or write a disciplinary referral because the child was almost certain to be punished more severely at home over what he/she had done in school.

"Then, as attitudes began to lighten up a little, when a child received a referral, the parent would either call the teacher, or request a meeting to go over what the child had done, and hear both sides of the story.

"There's nothing wrong with this in and of itself. It's good that parents took an interest in the discipline. However, this devolved into a situation where the parent would take the attitude of 'My child says he didn't do it,' where the word of children, who were not necessarily dishonest, but were at the developmental level where they would lie for fear of punishment, was taken over the word of the teacher.

"Often, when there were witnesses, we would hear phrases like, 'My daughter says they're all lying.'

"This led to a 'My child says it, I believe it, that settles it' mentality on the part of many parents.

"From there, it devolved into a situation of threats of lawsuits, crusading parents taking an 'unreasonable teacher' to the school board, etc. It reached a point where teachers were almost afraid to write referrals because the backlash was going to be so severe. And, alas, it created a generation of children whose parents literally refused to allow their children to be held responsible for anything; therefore, they grew up without a sense of responsibility."

The other consequence of modern living is that, in the last quarter of the 20th century, we evolved into a litigious society.

It started out legitimately enough: people would read a newspaper and see others being awarded large sums of money because, say, an insurance company tried to cheat them out of their rightful compensation. This "free money" mentality permeated society where everyone was looking for an excuse to sue everyone else.

Whereas the legal system was originally created to make people responsible for their actions, it instead went awry and made people less responsible.

For example, in one incident, an individual went crazy and started shooting at people in a library. It was necessary for police officers to take his life in the performance of their duty to protect innocent citizens.

His family then filed a lawsuit against the library district, claiming that if they would have had adequate security, the man wouldn't have been able to run wild and had to forfeit his life.

In short, the entire past 20 years has been a conditioning process for members of society to aggressively avoid accepting responsibility.

Responsibility to Family and/or Society

One of the reasons that the human race is the dominant species on the planet is a sense of community. This sense of community makes us feel responsible to the rest of society.

Even the most hardened brute, when crossing the street and seeing a little old lady stumble, will instinctively offer a hand to help her to her feet. Therefore, the natural human condition is to be responsible for one's fellow humans; to be irresponsible toward them is learned behavior.

The individual who blames others for the most insignificant things, like leaving the milk out of the refrigerator or leaving the cap off the toothpaste is looking for someone else to blame because he feels inadequate. He feels that by constantly calling attention to others' mistakes, he's diverting attention away from his own shortcomings or errors.

How many readers have arrived at work a few minutes late only to have a coworker, in a seemingly innocent tone, let everyone know he's late ("Oh, George, I'm glad you didn't call in sick, I was worried about you," in a voice three times normal volume.) Chances are this individual is not the company's star performer.

Our job is to teach our children that they and they alone are responsible for their behaviors and actions. As parents, our purpose is to raise our children so that they become fully functional, independent adults. These are adults who can make decisions for themselves and accept the consequences for those decisions.

Responsibility for Choices

A person who grows up without a sense of responsibility for choices is a person who is stifled in life. A person who is unwilling to take responsibility for choices avoids making choices whenever possible.

Haven't you met countless people who bounce ideas off of you and ask you for your opinion when, in reality they want you to choose for them. Then, if your advice backfires, they make a comment like, "This is all your fault. Why did I listen to you?" They're passing the responsibility off on you when, in fact, it you were an uninvolved third party.

Ever notice how some people, when you ride in the car with them, will sit there at a stop sign and not know whether to turn right or left? They pull over to the side of the road, pull out the map book, and consult it. That's because these people are subconsciously, due to conditioning, afraid to make a mistake.

Ever notice how others just turn right and, if the street numbers are progressing in the wrong direction, just flip a U-turn and go back the other way.

Their attitude is, "Yes, I made a wrong turn, and who cares?"

You accomplish the instillation of responsibility in your child by helping him recognize that mistakes are simply a part of life. We learn and grow from mistakes.

To succeed, you're going to have to go over some bumps, you're going to spill some milk, and you're going to fail. By allowing your child to go through this process without making the child feel inadequate for being human and fallible, we are teaching them that it's okay to make a wrong turn as long as they learn from the experience.

By having a child who can acknowledge his/her shortcomings, to admit to mistakes, to be unafraid of contrary opinions, you are molding an individual with a sense of responsibility. Love your children for their imperfections.

Responsibility for Possessions

Learning respect for material things is a part of learning responsibility. It's important that you teach your child that things that belong to him and others are to be respected and not to be mistreated.

To do this you have to walk a fine line. On the one hand, if your child breaks something and you immediately replace it, he won't value it. A better response to say, "Oh, I'm sorry it got broken, but it will be a while before we can afford to buy you another one."

This allows him to learn that when he breaks something he has to do without it for a while. This teaches him what it's like to be without it. As a result he'll value the replacement more highly.

When teaching this attribute a parent is responsible for measuring the motivation behind a child's treatment of possessions.

If a child breaks something, it can be for one of three reasons:

a) It's an accident (human error)

b) Carelessness (not paying attention or indifferent), or

c) Maliciousness (a deliberate act of destruction).

Once you've assessed their motivation then you can respond accordingly. If it's an accident, it must be stressed that accidents happen to everybody, but the object is still broken.

For example your child is playing and his elbow accidently knocks his milk over. You say, "Let me help you clean up the milk".

If the object was broken through carelessness, an element of teaching the child to be more careful (i.e., respectful) of things must be added to the response. For example he's play with his toys in the living room and steps on one of his favorites, breaking it. You might say, "I see you've broken your toy. It will be a while before we'll be able to buy another one".

If the act was malicious, sometimes punishment is appropriate, depending on the circumstances.

If, for example, Billy takes a baseball bat to his little television set, it's going to be a good long time before he ever has his own television again.

However, if Billy was angry at another child and kicked the leg of his dresser and his television set fell, you might consider allowing him to "work off" replacement cost by doing extra chores.

What's essential here is uncovering the source of the child's outburst. Is it a bid for attention, anger at a sibling, a problem at school? Understanding where the root cause is coming from allows you to deal with the underlying issue.

Responsibility for Other's Possessions

Respect for others' possessions is also important. For example, if your child breaks something that belongs to someone else and you try to teach him how it feels by breaking something of his, you're actually teaching him to avoid responsibility. That's because in the future it's a good bet that he won't admit to having broken something if no one knows he did it.

If you take an approach like, "Well, you made a mistake, don't blame yourself, but we can't let poor Tommy be without his bike," then you replace Tommy's bike, you're not giving your child the opportunity to take responsibility for his actions.

To teach your child responsibility it's perfectly okay to have them perform extra chores to "work off" the cost for Tommy's new bike. You don't want to overdo it here saying "No allowance for six months" but you certainly don't want to under do it either with a response like, "I'm docking you ten dollars from your allowance."

By giving them an amount, "That bike cost $80" and allowing them to work it off "You can earn $10 extra a week washing my car", your child learns that there is a consequence for being irresponsible, but that, if he takes responsibility, the situation is fixable. This way he learns to take responsibility for his future actions.

A Responsible Child is an Empowered Child

"You cannot escape the responsibility of tomorrow by evading it today."

- Abraham Lincoln

Technically, responsibility simply means "The ability to respond."

I think of responsibility as "the ability to choose our responses", in other words - response-ability.

In any of life's challenges, opportunities or disasters, we can respond in whatever way we choose. Responsibility is being accountable for your actions, and, for the most part, the quality of your life is determined by how much you, the individual, are willing to accept the responsibility for shaping it.

In the martial arts we stress that responsibility is a basic fundamental of training. As you read in the introduction, many outside the field find it a paradox that something that looks like, to the unenlightened eye, fighting, is totally the opposite of fighting.

The core of this belief is taking personal responsibility for one's life.

A martial artist is training to be "larger than life" or "greater than the sum of his/her" parts on a physical, mental and spiritual level. The net result will be fighting skills, accompanied by the responsibility that goes with those skills.

The reason people with these skills become such productive citizens is because of the price with which these skills are attained, and the responsibility that the attainment of these skills requires.

Students are responsible for attending classes regularly, for learning the material, for practicing on their own, etc. As they progress in rank and begin to teach the lower belts, they become responsible for their students. Every step of the way brings them added responsibility, in a slow, step-by-step process.

In a society where people have been raised with, quite literally, training in how to avoid responsibility, a child armed with a sense of responsibility is going to have a definite competitive advantage.

CHAPTER 5

Motivation

"What lies behind us and what lies before us are tiny matters compared to what lies within us."

- Ralph Waldo Emerson

Motivation can be defined in a multitude of ways. However, for our purposes we are going to distinguish between two forms of motivation: motivation for the parent and motivation for the child.

For the parent, motivation is getting children to behave in a way that they might not naturally want to behave or do things they might not want to do if left on their own. The way you motivate your child is all important; it gives him/her reasons to listen to you or not to listen to you, to clean her room or not to clean her room, to do his homework or not to do his homework.

For the child, motivation means having reasons to behave in a certain manner or do certain things, or to not behave in a certain manner or not do certain things.

For example, she might clean her room because she's trying to avoid punishment, or she might clean up her room because she anticipates a reward. Hopefully, with your help, she'll clean up her room because she has become committed to keeping his room clean.

An example of proper motivation occurred recently when I was conversing over the phone with a single mother. As we talked, I overheard her son talking to her in the background. This was early in the morning.

All of a sudden I heard him say, "I'm gonna wash clothes now."

To put this in perspective, her son is 11 years old. Now it's highly unusual, at that hour of the morning, that a son would tell his mother his intention to wash clothes in the same tone of voice he would use as if he were saying, "I'm going over to my friend Tommy's house."

This tweaked my interest so I questioned her as to how she motivated him to wash his clothes.

"I buy my kids certain clothes that they like," she replied, "with the understanding that if I do they're responsible for keeping them neat and clean. I taught them how to wash clothes, and that's become part of the package."

In other words, she motivated her children by purchasing them clothes and they became committed to keeping and wearing clean clothes. This also taught them responsibility for their possessions (see the last chapter).

As parents and teachers, we need to help children choose a path that will take them toward their goals and beyond. That's the importance of knowing how to motivate your children and helping them learn how to motivate themselves.

Motivation is the start of all success and failure in life. It is actually putting your thoughts into action.

With proper motivation, your child can achieve much more in her life and be inspired to continue to set higher and higher targets for which to reach. Motivation will cause her to stretch and work to and past her present perceived limitations. Her motivation will give her the drive she needs for personal excellence in all areas of her life.

Types of Motivation

How can we become motivated?

Motivation has two basic contrasting ("flip-side") traits:

1. Is the motivation internal or external?

Some people are motivated by rewards, such as money or trophies. Children can be motivated through gifts, stickers, praise, or grades in school. They can also be motivated by punishments such as restrictions, time outs, removal of privileges or spankings. Psychologists call these external motivators.

External motivation is also known as incentive. Incentive is generally a reward or punishment. Your incentive for not beating up someone who annoys you is that you don't want to end up in jail. Your incentive for working overtime is you want more money.

Internal motivation is when you do something because the resulting good feelings you receive about yourself is important to you. For example you may donate money to cancer research or volunteer your time at an abuse clinic because you feel it's our duty to help those less fortunate than ourselves. Your donation gives you a feeling of congruousness, making you feel how you like you feel yourself. Psychologists call internal motivation.

You don't help because you expect a reward or fear punishment. You just want to do something because you feel it's the right thing to do. It also gives you a good feeling about yourself.

2. Is the motivation positive or negative?

Positive motivation, by way of example, might be recognition; that is, when people tell us what a good job we've done or we receive an award or bonus of some kind.

A positive motivator for a child might be getting a treat for doing something exceptionally well, or being named student of the month. It is important, however, to realize that if we are the ones dispensing positive motivators, the reward of positive motivation is for something above and beyond normal expectations, not for simply meeting expectations.

For an intelligent student, a reward for getting an "A" is rewarding him simply for meeting normal expectations. For a student who is not naturally gifted and has difficulty working at the "C" level, getting an "A" requires a great deal of effort above and beyond expectations. This behavior is worthy of a reward.

Negative motivation is motivation by such things as avoidance of punishment, avoidance of ridicule by other students, of not having friends if the child behaves poorly, etc. A negative motivator is a behavior you try to avoid because of the potentially negative consequences you receive from these behaviors.

In the adult world, a positive motivator for not telling lies about someone is you realize that it's wrong and it hurts the other person. A negative motivator is the fear of a lawsuit. Negative motivators for children could be the aforementioned punishments.

All motivators have their purpose. The fact that we live in a society of laws is evidence that we're all subject to negative motivation.

The motivation of getting arrested if caught stealing will keep most people honest. That's useful negative motivation.

What would be even more useful would be the positive motivation of not stealing because you don't want to take something from a person because you know that person worked hard to get that thing.

Let's examine the different types of motivators and how they affect your children.

Internal and External Motivation

As we've already discussed, external motivation comes from outside of us. It is neither good nor bad in and of itself and many external motivators serve useful purposes.

For example, I've referred to motivation as being something that makes a person behave in a way they would not naturally behave if left to their own devices.

Working, for example, is not a natural motivation. Humans tend to be lazy by nature and invariably seek the path of least resistance (easiest route). Successful inventors are inventors who create things that make life easier.

Human beings are unique in the animal kingdom in that they work. Every other animal, except beasts of burden (who are impressed into labor by humans), lives a simple existence of basically lounging around and searching for food when they get hungry. They only expend energy to get energy.

Early in human evolution, nature provided everything. Fruits and vegetables on trees, natural shelter, etc.

However, as human beings began to venture into less hospitable climates, clothing became necessary, and human hands had to make it. Food sources became less plentiful, and it took work to look for and attain food.

This created a situation unique to our species. The more we went against our natural tendency toward expending minimum effort, the more we attained. Thus was born a basic law of human nature: The greater the motivation, the greater the achievement.

Internal motivation is when the reason we do things is motivated by personal desire which comes from within. We are not necessarily expecting an immediate reward because of our behavior. This does not mean that we never expect some kind of recognition or reward for our behavior.

When a woman goes to work in a profession she enjoys, much of the reward she receives come from the doing, the satisfaction of her accomplishments. In other words, she's doing the work and doing it well because she enjoys it. That's good and it's important.

For example, say the woman is a biologist. She is coming up with different ways of tracking the genetic chain. It's stimulating and she's well paid. She thinks that the reason she's doing this is so that, in conjunction with other biologists, she can come up with cures to certain genetic illnesses, such as breast cancer.

Now, let's say the woman finds out that the work she's doing is secretly being funded by the government, and the results she's getting are part of a project to find out a way to eliminate people with blue eyes from the population because the government doesn't like people with blue eyes.

She, hopefully (because I happen to have blue eyes) would be motivated internally to find another position, one that fits in more with her internal values. This is an internal motivation; when you are motivated by a set of feelings and values within yourself.

Both internal and external motivations are important. Both are used to get ourselves and our children to do what we want them to do. We are motivated somewhat externally to go to work to support ourselves and our families. But we are also motivated internally because we want the best for our families, and we want our children to have advantages in life. While this isn't something we necessarily get strokes for it is something we feel is very important.

Positive and Negative Motivators

Motivation has also been defined as pulling or drawing out what is inside. There are two diametrically opposed types of motivation: positive and negative.

To restate simply: positive motivators are motivators that make us want to do something.

Positive motivators can be thought of as motivators that pull your children toward certain behaviors. Positive motivation is when your child feels good about what will happen when he or she does something. This is usually some type of reward or good feeling that comes as a result of completing a task or chore.

Negative motivation is when your child will feel bad about doing, or not doing something.

This can be thought of as motivation that pushes your child away from certain behaviors. This might be when you give your child a time out for not listening or when you take away her privilege of having friends visit when she doesn't clean her room.

In short, negative motivation makes your child try hard to avoid an anticipated outcome in a situation. Positive motivation makes him try to attain a certain outcome in a situation.

Suppose you want Johnny to clean his room. He hasn't been doing a real great job of this, so you sit him down and discuss with him why it's important to have a clean room.

You tell him it makes things easier to find, gives him pride in himself and his room, it keeps harmony in the family, and it shows that he cares about his home and family. Johnny agrees in principle, but is still negligent and, perhaps even lazy about it. In other words, he's unmotivated.

So, since Johnny's really into baseball, you tell him that if he can keep his room immaculate for one week, you'll take him to the ball game.

This does the trick. He's enthused and keeps his room clean, and you have a great time at the game.

But what happens if Johnny doesn't keep it clean the week after? Are you now going to offer him season tickets to keep his room clean? No way!

The big problem with this type of external motivation is that it rewards the child for performing up to expectation, and often doesn't make the person want to change their behavior pattern. On the other hand, if it does work, and by getting this reward Johnny starts to keep his room clean because you've gotten him to form a new habit, it was well worth it.

A negative motivator might be something like, "Johnny, if you don't clean up this mess you'll never see another ball game again."

Now, Johnny likes baseball, so he cleans his room out of fear. Your motivation has worked, or has it?

Well, maybe temporarily, but it's teaching Johnny to clean his room not for his own reasons, but to clean it to keep on dad's good side so he can go to the game. The problem with this is as soon as the game is no longer an issue, or if dad isn't around he'll lapse into his old behavior.

The idea is to motivate Johnny to become responsible for his own actions. That takes positive motivation.

Let's look at some ways to replace negative motivation with positive motivation.

Negative Motivators and Positive Replacements

Negative motivators are motivators such as punishments, sanctions, threats and nagging. There are obviously others.

Let's take a look at the most common, threats, first.

Replacing Threats

Threats are one way to help your child turn off to almost anything you say. Many parents will say things like, "If you keep that up, I'm going to swat you!" or "If you do that one more time you'll be grounded for a month!"

We say this not because we have any intention of carrying out the threats but because we're hoping the children will believe them and "knock it off." The problem is that children are very discerning and will know that you're "all bark and no bite."

Threats merely undermine your credibility. A GIANT rule to remember is NEVER THREATEN! Threats are utterly without value.

One way to replace threats is to promise a result that will make both you and your child happy. Put a positive spin on the situation.

When your child isn't getting ready to leave the house when you leave, instead of threatening ("Get ready right now or I'll drag you out!") say, "Hey, if you hurry up we'll have time to go to the pet shop and check out the new puppies after we drop my papers off at the office."

If you're at the grocery store and your child is begging for treats (that they strategically place so the children can readily see them), instead of threatening, "If you don't stop whining about those Gummy Bears I'll give you a spanking right here," tell her, "I'll tell you what. Put those back and when we get home I'll let you help me make some popcorn." Not only have you diverted her attention, but you're giving her a healthier treat.

The idea is to motive your child toward the desired behavior. By emphasizing the positive and giving your child a logical reason to do something, the child will more likely do what you need him/her to do. This is especially helpful with smaller children.

Punishment of Consequence

Another replacement for the threat is the "punishment of consequence." This isn't a direct punishment; it isn't a punishment you inflict. It's a punishment which occurs as a result of cause and effect.

For example, if your child uses his boom box for a football and wrecks it, you certainly don't run out and replace it. A natural consequence for mistreating his boom box is that now he has to live without one.

This can also be effective in teaching responsibility, consideration and punctuality.

If, for example, you are going somewhere and the child wants to accompany you, you might say, "Be ready in half an hour." If your child then deliberately stalls (children do frequently test parents this way) and isn't ready in half an hour, you leave without him.

This teaches your child that you mean what you say, and that if he doesn't adhere to the agreement, he misses out. Again, it impresses upon your child that there are consequences for wrong behavior as a result of the natural flow of events.

In the chapter on self-discipline, the topic of punishment is dealt with quite extensively. It would be repetitive to go over the punishment topic twice in the same book. However, we feel that punishments of various forms are essential to instilling a sense of consequence in children.

The sense of consequence is also directly tied to a sense of responsibility. This is not to imply that children should be conditioned, like dogs receiving electric shocks for wrong choices, by punishment for wrong behavior. The conditioning consists of making the child realize that if a negative act is performed, there will be a negative reaction.

Alternatives to Punishment

As we have discussed, punishment is a measure for dealing with unacceptable behavior. The problem is that, the first time you put Joey in time out for talking back to you, you've just made him angry.

There is a good chance he'll repeat the behavior with more flair. Now you' become angry. You'll have to escalate, which could mean (we do not recommend this but it does happen) you decide to give him a swat on the butt.

Joey will escalate too, only this time it'll be at the grocery store or someplace else where you will be caused embarrassment and consternation. It's also a place where you will think twice about using a swat on the butt.

What can a good parent do?

One of the best things you can do in cases like this is to ask questions. By asking questions you actually teach your child the desired behavior in a way he/she can understand it.

When your child talks back to you (supposed you have family rules set up as in the discipline section) you ask your child something like, "Kathy, why do we have family rules?"

Kathy says something like "I don't know" or "I guess so we can all get along."

Whatever it is, after you've established the reason your family has for its rules you can say something like, "How do you think I feel when you talk to me like you just did?" (We're assuming that you've kept your cool during this incident.)

"Well you probably felt bad/got mad (or whatever)."

The important thing here is not the words. The important thing is that you're helping your child think through a situation, putting him/herself in the place of another person. In this case you're helping your child develop empathy (the ability to feel as another person feels, compassion, sensitivity, and so on).

Let's ask an important question here: What's your long-term goal for this child? Is your long- term goal to make him instantly obedient to anyone in authority? Probably not.

There was a highly publicized instance in Japan which was the result of a generation bred to immediately recognize authority and submit to it without question. A group of men dressed as doctors walked into a bank with medicine bottles, and told the employees they had to be inoculated against radiation poisoning from the atomic bombs (dropped nearly 50 years previously). Everyone assumed they were trained medical specialists, and submitted to the shots.

The shots, in fact, contained a powerful sedative which put all the employees to sleep. The men then robbed the bank at leisure, without resistance.

In other words, people who are conditioned to instantly submit to authority are generally at the mercy of those who are not. They are content to be in service positions and to let others do the thinking. In modern vernacular they are "suckers."

In a famous social psychological study performed by Yale University psychologist Stanley Milgram during the 1960's, students were recruited reportedly for a learning experiment. The experiment had three participants, an Experimenter, a Teacher and a Learner or Student.

The Student and Experimenter were actually actors, hired to be part of the experiment. The teacher was a randomly assigned subject who didn't have any idea what the experiment was actually about.

In reality the experiment was to understand why seemingly normal German soldiers repeatedly performed the horrendous acts they did in World War II. After discovering these horrendous acts the Germans told Allied authorities that they were "only following orders". The experiment was to see if "normal people" would actually follow orders that could result in injury to another person.

The two actors would meet with the subject in a laboratory room. The Experimenter would tell the two "subjects" that they were going to be part of a learning experiment and then had then select a piece of paper that was supposedly to assign one of them randomly to the role of "Teacher" and the other to "Student". The actor that was to become the "Learner" would always proclaim they had selected the paper with "Learner" on it.

The students were brought into a room which contained what appeared to be an electronic control panel, with a knob. Voltage readings were around the knob. The readings started at a low number and increased (so the subjects thought) as the knob was turned to the right.

At the extreme right the numbers were painted red and there was a warning, "Danger Level! Can Cause Serious Injury to Death!"

The students were then told that when the "Learner" made a mistake they were to turn the knob to the right, increasing the voltage with every incorrect answer. They were then given a small shock at a low voltage so they would understand that the shocks would hurt.

In reality there was no voltage hooked to the student, they just acted as if they were shocked when the switch was pulled.

At first the actor would pretend that the shocks were uncomfortable but not serious, but as the voltage increased they would begin to shout and scream as if in pain. They would say things such as "Please, no more" and other such things.

If the "Teacher" became confused and asked what they should do or stopped the "Experimenter" would say, "The experiment requires that you continue" and other similar things.

When Milgram set up this experiment he postulated that less than 4 percent of the "Teachers" would actually continue into the dangerous levels above 300 volts. He assumed that the students would draw the line when the pain got to a certain level, but that's not what happened.

What he found was unsettling. Fully 65 percent of the students continued to turn the voltage up even when the culprit was yelling and screaming for mercy as long as the "Experimenter" continued to say "The experiment requires that you continue."

What has this to do with listening to authority? Everything! People who do not learn to think for themselves tend to take the easy way out and depend on others to make their decisions.

Remember our example of the friend who's always asking you "What do you think I should do?" This is an extreme example of how people who don't want to think for themselves can be convinced by those in authority to do all kinds of atrocious things.

Although the experiment was performed to see why Nazi death camp guards would do what they did, it actually proved that most people bow to authority because they have never internalized their own set of values.

What has this to do with your child? Probably your long-term goal for your child is to help him or her become self-motivated and self-disciplined. You're trying to help your child become self- responsible, to act on his/her own internalized set of values.

You don't want your child swayed by the crowd or popular opinion, but rather to be led by what he or she believes is right. That's why asking questions is so important! By asking questions you're focusing on the long-term solution, making your child think about what is important. You are helping your child become self-motivated, self-disciplined and self-driven.

The same is true of telling or nagging. Instead of telling or nagging, ask your children questions that get them focused on what is motivating them.

When you tell your child "Stop hitting your brother! Why do I always have to tell you that?" you are, in essence, telling your child "You can't think for yourself, you have no self-control and the only way I can motivate you is by nagging you and telling you what to do!"

Can you think of anyone who would be positively motivated in this manner? What did I do just now? I asked you a question. What a coincidence!

Now, of course, the obvious question you could ask is "Why are you always hitting your brother?"

This is a small step in the right direction, but you'll probably get a response like, "He bugs me!"

Now you need to understand the answer to the next obvious question, why does he "bug" him? Does he deliberately irritate him or does his mere existence "bug" older brother? If you follow this line of reasoning it leads to the lecture about how it's not right to hit someone over "bugging" you.

This is the time to try empathy. Why not ask your child, "How do you think your brother feels when you hit him?"

He'll probably answer with something like, "Well, bad, I guess."

"How do you feel when someone bigger than you hits you?"

"Bad, really bad," would probably be an example of his reply.

"What do you think you should do about this?"

"Well, I guess I shouldn't hit him," goes the potential response.

"When a bigger kid hits you, would you feel better if he apologized?"

"Well, yeah," comes the answer. "I guess I should tell him I'm sorry."

Now, of course, there's no such thing as an ideal world. You'll have to tune your response to the degree of rebelliousness you experience or your child's responses.

This is not a "If he says this, you do that" set of guidelines. Just as children must think for themselves, so must parents.

But this is an example of how to set the direction of the solution using questions and empathy. It will also help your child to put himself in other people's shoes. This will help them think through their choices. It also helps them think about the consequences.

In other words, it will help your become more self-motivated.

One phrase to be avoided at all costs, when your child strikes another child, is "What did he do?"

The naturally curious response as to what triggered the child's reaction often just slips out. But by asking your child this question, you're subliminally (and not so subliminally) telling him that certain actions would justify physical attack.

In martial arts classes, a child will frequently "act out" by not following directions. This could consist of treating a senior student disrespectfully, making fun of another student, making faces, daydreaming, etc.

A good instructor will take the child aside and say, kindly, "Tommy, why are you here?"

The response will usually be, "To learn karate (or tae kwon do, or Tang Soo Do or kung-fu)."

"What's your goal in training with us?"

The reply will almost always be, "To become a black belt."

"How do you become a black belt?"

Some typical answers are, "By listening," or "By training hard," or "By being good."

Then it's time to ask a question that focuses the child on their long-term behavior.

"If you want to be a black belt, how hard should you try? Should you try your best or just try to get by?"

"I should try my best!" is always the reply.

"Are you trying your best right now?"

The answer will generally (and almost always) be a very sheepish negative. However, you end up with a re-motivated and fired-up student, behaving well because now they are trying to be their best.

This is accomplished simply by asking questions that help the child focus on their long term objective. They want to achieve the rank of black belt.

This process isn't unique to martial arts. It can be applied to anything.

First, determine, with the help of a child, what they wants.

Maybe she does poorly on a math test. You could tell your child, "How are you going to get into college with grades like this?"

I promise you, this will do little to motivate him (I've tried it). The facts are very few children are motivated by the thought of spending (to them) an eternity in school.

On the other hand, you could ask your child some questions that will help them view their future in a way that involves doing better math.

"What do you want to be when you grow up, Sally?"

Sally replies: "An astronaut!"

"What do astronauts do?"

You'll get different answers, but you can flow with the conversation in a way to steer it to let your child see why his math grade today is important.

"Do you think the astronauts need to use math when they're doing those experiments on the space shuttle?"

"Sure. They probably have to figure out a lot of things."

"Sally, do you know that on the moon the gravity is only 1/16 the gravity on earth. Can you tell me how much you'd weigh on the moon?"

In other words, you've gotten through to him, by way of her dreams of the future, the importance of learning math.

The next step is, of course, to say something like, "Well, you know astronauts have to be really good in math. You seem to be having a little trouble with math. What can I do to help?"

You've just used three simple steps that involve questioning that you can always use to help your child become more internally motivated:

1. You found out, through questions, what motivates your child. You figured out what goals your child has. In this case, it was becoming an astronaut (at least for the moment).
2. You helped your child realize, through questions, that working in this area is important to his/her goals. Here you demonstrated that an astronaut needs to be good in math.
3. This last thing you did was ask your child what you could do to help. In this example, you might tutor your child or arrange for a professional math tutor to help your child through this rough patch.

You might help your child schedule his/her homework and/or help them set homework goals. You can, again, set these goals through questions.

When we nag or tell constantly, it's a turn-off to our children, spouses, coworkers, employees, just about everyone.

I can't ever think of a time when I've been motivated by someone telling me what to do; can you? By using questions you help your child develop internal motivations for doing what needs to be done for them to be successful in every area of their lives.

Let's take a look at another example, doing the dishes.

Doing the dishes is your son's chore. He knows it. He doesn't do it.

You try bribes, nagging, punishment; the dishes still don't get done. So you sit him down and have a conversation with him.

"Son, why is it that we need the dishes done?"

The amount of negative energy that you've both expended so far into this will determine what his answer will be. But let's assume he's not deeply entrenched into this behavior and not doing the dishes is not his way of "making a stand." He just doesn't like doing the dishes.

Let's also assume that you have family rules that have been worked out and agreed upon in family meetings. One of the rules is your son does the dishes on Monday, Wednesday and Friday nights.

"We do the dishes so they're clean."

"And why is this important?"

"Oh, so we don't get a bunch of germs and get all sick and stuff."

You can then follow up with, "And what about the family rules."

"Well, yeah. When I do the dishes the house runs smoother."

You can now ask: "And do you think it's fair that doing the dishes is your chore on your nights?"

"Well, yeah. I just wish Karen was old enough to do more."

You've just discovered that there is some resentment about a younger sibling who appears, to your son, not to be pulling her weight. This is something you can address now, along with any other issues which might come up.

The point is that you've just helped your son realize the reasons for doing the dishes on his own. You didn't tell him why it was necessary. You got him to tell you why.

This moves your child a lot closer toward self-motivation than all the nagging or threats in the world could. You're looking for motivation that will last.

You can choose motivation for the short term which is telling, controlling, rewarding and punishing. The problem with this is that it is external and short term in focus.

You can also choose motivation for the long term which includes what is acceptable behavior through family rules. This, combined with questions, will help focus your child on the results of their acts which will motivate them internally. It will give your child internal commitment.

Kids, and adults, for that matter, will do infinitely more through internal rather than external motivation.

When your child discovers that she has the answers, she also has the ownership of those answers. She becomes more responsible and her self-esteem and self-confidence will soar.

We have now taught our child to be self-motivated toward self-discipline. Now the final step is to put some self-responsibility into that self-disciplined motivation.

CHAPTER 6

Enthusiasm

"Action and feeling go together."
- William James

Enthusiasm is essentially a combination of high energy and dedication. When someone takes on a task with zeal they are said to be "enthusiastic." It is also highly contagious.

People aren't persuaded by what we say, but by what they understand and feel. People around us are going to feel the same way we feel.

People are never persuaded by our words. They are persuaded by how we are saying what we are saying.

Actors have a saying, "It's all in the delivery."

For example, a simple line like, "Yeah, right" can be taken in an infinite number of ways. If you walk up to someone and say, "You're a doctor, aren't you" and he says, "Yeah, right," he's telling you that you guessed correctly.

If a person is having difficulty with the solution to a difficult problem and you make a suggestion, "It might work if you try this," and his eyes light up and he says, "Yeah, right!" he's telling you you've just helped him and he agrees with you.

If you tell someone "You look good in that outfit" and she replies, "Yeah, right," she's sarcastically telling you she disagrees and she believes your words are insincere. Again, just a tiny bit of inflection makes a world of difference.

People can sense your enthusiasm.

If you're less than enthusiastic about a task, people know on an instinctive level. You betray it in a number of different ways, from your body language to your tone of voice.

A leader has to transfer their knowledge and feeling to get the desired, positive result. How do they accomplish this? Enthusiasm is the key.

Your sense of enthusiasm in regard to your children is all-important. If Johnny comes home and shows you an "A" on his report card where there had been a "C" on his previous card, he'll immediately know whether or not you're sincerely happy about his improvement by your enthusiasm level.

If your answer is "Gee, that's good," and you turn back to your work table, it's going to send an entirely different message than "Wow, that's quite an improvement! Congratulations!" accompanied by a high five and eyes beaming with pride.

Your children will also inherit, not through genetics but through environmental conditioning, your enthusiasm level.

If you're always complaining about the boss, work, etc., you'll have a child who will be less than enthusiastic about work. If you're always complaining about your friends, you'll have a child who will be less than enthusiastic about friendships.

If mom and dad are always complaining about each other behind each others' backs -- that's right! The next generation will be less than enthusiastic about relationships.

The Three Types of People

There are three types of people:

1. Those who make it happen.
2. Those who watch it happen.
3. Those who wake up the next morning and say, "Gee. What happened?"

If you're going to raise a successful and happy child, you want a child who's not content to sit back and watch the parade. Your child must want to be a part of the parade or, better yet, lead it.

Teaching Enthusiasm

Unfortunately, enthusiasm is one attribute that can't be taught by strategy. A person can't learn enthusiasm.

A person can only be, for lack of a better term, "infected" with it.

You have to be an enthusiastic person to raise enthusiastic children. Of course, this is a very general rule, a special friend or teacher or even sibling might be the stimulus for enthusiasm, but usually, the burden will rest on you, the parent.

What does it take to become an enthusiastic person? Well, it comes from within; it's an inner attitude of true enjoyment or happiness.

You have to be excited that you are alive. You need to look for the good instead of the bad in each day.

It is often said, "Successful people do the things that failures won't because successful people realize that they have to get done."

So to feel enthusiastic, act enthusiastic. Be excited and animated.

Enthusiasm Motivators

Enthusiasm is an internal motivator. It is a joyous excitement.

Most children are overwhelmed by enthusiasm during the approach of a favorite holiday. What parent hasn't noted the change in energy level and zeal during times of year considered particularly joyous? This type of enthusiasm is called "anticipatory" because it is created by the anticipation of something happy or positive.

The general idea in instilling enthusiasm, therefore, is to create and maintain this anticipatory feeling toward goal achievement.

"Just think of what it's going to be like to set foot on the campus your first day of college... the autumn air, the ivy, the beginning of the rest of your life."

Such a statement goes a long way toward helping your child on a number of fronts: it reinforces internal motivation, it reinforces goal setting, it helps your child visualize a desired result, and it creates a sense of enthusiasm.

Another way of maintaining enthusiasm is to have a pep talk with yourself. Write down the reasons why you are confident you can do something, why you want to do it, and what the results will be. This will increase your excitement level.

When people around you see that you are excited, they will become excited as well.

When you lead with logic, but no emotion, you leave your associates well-educated, but not very enthusiastic. They are not emotionally involved.

The same can be said of your children. They may respond to your words, but they'll be quicker to respond to your feelings. Using a balance of logic and emotion will make you a people builder.

Remember, excited people get things done!

CHAPTER 7

Self-Confidence

Self-confidence is feeling sure of yourself. For example, if you've ever played basketball, it's that sensation you feel when you're shooting from the free throw line and you know you can make the shot.

Self-confidence can help you be successful with something you haven't done before. When a bully threatens your child, you child can let him push them around or take their lunch money, or they can use their self-confidence to stand up to him without fighting.

Self-Confidence Helps You Stand Up to Your Fears

Fears are what you feel: that clutching feeling you have any time you don't believe in yourself. You can be afraid or fearful of the dark, or you can be fearful of talking in front of people, or you might be fearful of a subject in school.

For you to do anything, it is important to beat your fears and practice self-confidence.

Self-confidence is also a sense of certainty, a belief that you can take on any challenge in your environment. It is also a belief that you can be successful at a task or in a situation that you've never had to deal with before.

Self-confidence empowers you to stand up to fear, put it behind you, and see new challenges as an exciting adventure.

Being a leader will often bring you into situations where you can't be certain of the outcome. You have to be able to face these unpredictable situations with confidence because the people following your lead won't follow someone who is afraid. Being self-confident helps you become a true leader.

Ways to Improve Self-Confidence

Positive Self Talk

One way to improve your self-confidence is talking positively to yourself. This is known as positive self talk.

When people make mistakes they often use negative self talk. They say things like, "I can't believe I'm so stupid!" or "You're such a moron! How could you do that?"

Instead you can use positive self talk. You can tell yourself something like "Next time I'll do better. I can learn from this mistake."

After you frame your mistake as a learning experience you can think about what you learned from the mistake. By teaching yourself to talk positively to yourself, and redefining mistakes as learning experiences, you can greatly enhance your self-confidence level.

Visualization

You can also improve your confidence through a process called "visualization." Visualization is a process used by athletes, doctors, actors and just about anyone who performs at a high level.

For example, athletes play movies over and over in their heads where they see themselves winning. This is visualization. Visualization is a fancy word that means using your imagination to picture yourself already having results you want.

To improve your self-confidence, picture yourself doing whatever it is that is causing your fear, and doing it well. See yourself doing the thing you are afraid of successfully, and soon you will succeed.

For example if you are afraid of speaking in front of groups of people, visualize yourself having fun while speaking in front of a large group of people.

Do What You Fear

To overcome your fear, you must do whatever is causing your fear or anxiety. By doing what you fear, you will start to become self-confident.

If doing a form in front of your martial arts class makes you nervous, get a friend, one you trust, to watch you do a form. After a while, you can ask other people to watch you do your form, which will improve your self-confidence. This is a step-by-step way of increasing your self-confidence.

Ask For Help

Another way to improve your self-confidence is to ask someone who knows how to do what you would like to do for advice or help. Going again to the example of a martial arts form, you can get a senior student or instructor to look at your form privately, then ask them to give you some pointers.

What you may find out is that you're actually doing a good job, but your anxiety about the situation gives you a poor self image of what you're doing. If you truly aren't doing well, then the person you asked can give you pointers on how to improve.

Think About Something You Do Well

One other way to improve your self-confidence is to think about or do something that you already do well before you take on the task that is causing you anxiety.

Using the martial arts form example (I promise this is the last time), do a form you feel that you do very well a couple of times. Now try doing the form of which you're not so sure.

You'll see success breeds confidence. By doing something successfully you will have more confidence in trying something new.

Improving Your Children's Self-Confidence through Communication - The Dangers of Mixed Messages and Criticism

Dr. Jean Yoder and William Proctor describe communication, or rather, "miscommunication" with a young child in their book "The Self-Confident Child." This preschooler, after working very hard to tie his shoes, goes in to show his father what he's done.

His father says, "That's great, but you should have made sure your shoes were on the right feet."

Notice the message here.

The father tells the child what he should have done. He is trying to make a better product instead of helping his child's feel better about his efforts. He is definitely not building this child's self-confidence.

When children are giving this kind of mixed message, where praise is mixed with criticism, the child will tend to focus on the criticism.

When your seven-year-old washes the dishes and proudly shows you how well he's done and you praise him for his work, but then you go and wipe some soap spots off of a couple of glasses, you're giving him a mixed message.

Your child is receiving, "Mommy said I did a good job, but it looks like I didn't."

This is the same danger we encounter in anything that gives our children input, such as sports.

For example, your 12-year-old daughter is on the team driving the ball toward the goal in a soccer game. She has the ball passed to her. She takes the shot and shanks it off of her foot.

She comes out of the game feeling dejected. You go up to her and say, "You should have taken more time to kick the ball..." You tell her everything she did wrong.

She doesn't need to hear that, especially right now.

What she needs is the ability to look at the situation as a way to improve, rather than as a failure. She doesn't need your "constructive criticism."

Since neither you nor your daughter can change the past, and nothing can take away the disappointment of the messed up shot, hold back on immediate feedback.

Later, in a more private setting, give your child the opportunity to discuss her feelings about messing up and the two of you can develop a plan to improve her kicking skills. This will greatly improve your child's self-confidence.

Teasing Isn't Funny

In an article in "Reader's Digest" by Harriet Webster, Ms. Webster points out how teasing by parents is the most painful form of teasing there is. She cites Dr. Carole Lieberman, a psychiatrist in Beverly Hills, California.

"Children look to their parents as a mirror to tell them who they are in this world," Dr. Lieberman explains. By teasing, the parent creates a sense of uncertainty about themselves because "a child never knows how serious a parent is."

We can all probably identify with this, some more than others.

One study conducted at group therapy sessions for men with histories of unsatisfactory relationships with women found that although many of these men were more attractive and successful than average, they had no self-confidence in dealing with the opposite sex. Over 80 percent of these men were subject to parental teasing during adolescent years.

A mother teasing a son about having an overbite or freckles might make him feel less than attractive. A father teasing a son about girls, "(Singing) Billy has a girl--friend! Billy has a girl--friend..." programs the child to repress displaying feelings toward a member of the opposite sex for fear of ridicule.

In Ms. Webster's study, she goes on to say that in a clinical study of 40 overweight women at the Yale Center for Eating and Weight Disorders in New Haven, Connecticut, researchers examined the relationship between self-confidence and being teased about weight and size. Those who reported a greater frequency of ridicule about their weight while growing up held a more negative view of their appearance as adults.

Self-confidence, when eroded, can be eroded for a lifetime.

For example, if your child shows signs of being nearsighted, if, on the way to the eye doctor you repeatedly say, "I hope he doesn't need glasses," if he does, indeed, require corrective lenses, he will feel that he is less than a child with 20/20 vision.

If, on the other hand, you say, "There's a chance you might see better with glasses, so we're going to get your eyes checked and if the doctor says you do, we'll pick out some really cool-looking frames" you're a lot less likely to have a child bumping into walls because he won't wear his glasses.

One classic anecdote occurred when the author of this book was having lunch in a restaurant with an all-you-can-eat salad bar. A gentleman who was at least 100 pounds overweight was at the next booth.

At a booth across the aisle, a boy who appeared to be about 13 was being chastised by his parents for not finishing his lunch. "You have to eat right," insisted his mother. "You're sooooo skinny!" "Tommy," the father joined in, "no girl is gonna look at you when you look like a rail."

At that, the portly gent looked over at the boy and said, "Listen to your folks, son. That's exactly what mine told me!"

Chapter 8

Courage

"We have nothing to fear but fear itself."
- Franklin Delano Roosevelt

Courage is an attribute misunderstood by most people. Courage is not the absence of fear. Courage is the ability to move forward in spite of your fear.

Fear is a natural instinct based on self-preservation. Without fear of getting run over and killed or seriously injured, we'd probably just venture into the street and get plowed over by oncoming traffic.

When a person is able to move forward in spite of his or her fears, that person is said to be courageous. A student who stands in front of class delivering a speech in spite of stage fright is courageous. A person who stands up to a bully in spite of his fear of the bully is courageous.

Fear is very stifling and can create a negative situation if it is not counterbalanced by courage. Bullies don't bully out of aggressive hostility, they bully out of fear. They are afraid of the world, so they seek to make more vulnerable individuals afraid of them.

Two words with opposite meanings are "hero" and "coward." The coward is not just paralyzed by fear; the coward is led to negative actions through fear, such as bullying. The hero is someone who perseveres in spite of fear.

Risk Taking

The reason courage is such an important factor with which to arm your child is because no one succeeds without taking risks. Learning to take conscious, calculated risks is a stepping stone to success.

Through risk taking, your child learns that losses, setbacks and failures are the only way to significantly improve. They learn through these experiences, just as they learn through their mistakes.

If you ask anyone to name a great baseball player, chances are the name "Babe Ruth" will spring back at you almost instantaneously. Babe Ruth was the champion home run hitter of his day, and became one of baseball's icons. The fact that his 1935 record of 714 home runs stood for many decades before Hank Aaron hit his 715th home run in 1974 attests to his greatness.

What most people don't realize is that Babe Ruth struck out 1,333 times during his career. Obviously, this didn't make him afraid to try again or, he tried again in spite of his fear of striking out.

Teaching Courage

Again, courage can't be taught. However, it can be encouraged. The main thing you can do to raise a courageous child is to convey the following:

1. Courage does not mean foolishness. It does not mean taking foolish risks, such as running across a crowded street.

    It also does not mean taking unnecessary risks to prove how brave you are to your peer group, such as violating the law or endangering yourself. Courage should never be confused with foolhardiness.

1. Sensible risks are the only way to advance in life. Even if you're afraid of the outcome, if you face that fear and attempt the task anyway, there is no way you're going to be a loser.

2. If you fail, you will have learned from failure. If you win, you will have attained your goal.

3. A person must be willing to risk temporary loss for the chance of permanent improvement.

4. The most successful people have a history of trying, failing, then picking themselves up and trying again.

You may also wish to share your adventures in your business career with your child. Although he or she might not understand the intricacies of what you do for a living, your child will appreciate the fact that you took a risk and then stuck to it, trying to achieve what you set out to do.

You can share how at first the outcome was negative, but the next time you "knew better." The lesson was you learned from the situation.

If the outcome was positive, this will also serve as an example to your child, showing them a positive pattern they might be able to use for themselves.

Hearing others tell about their risk-taking, and how they kept forging ahead in spite of their fears is very inspirational. Your stories encourage your child to take calculated, thought-out risks.

It is also important to encourage your child to admit his or her fears about something. Only a dysfunctional person is not afraid of anything, or refused to admit his/her fears.

Discussing a fear prior to an undertaking will be a fascinating and affirming admission for your newly emerging risk-taker. It will also help them build the courage they'll need the next time they have to do something new.

Facing Fears

In the martial arts field, we maintain a built-in fear-facing device. Many of the advanced techniques, such as black belt level moves, look far too complex and demanding to the new student.

A white belt might remark, "I'm afraid I'll never be able to do that kick."

This is easily countered by any black belt, who will respond, "I was afraid too when I was a white belt. But I learned to do it, and so will you."

All human beings tend to let their imaginations run away with them when it comes to fear. These imaginings are usually pure fantasy, a mental exaggeration of the worst thing that could happen. They almost never come to pass.

When you share your fantasies, especially the sillier ones, with your children, they understand that they're part of being human. And when you share with them that your fear never came to pass, you're teaching them that most fears are irrational fantasies that never materialize.

Say your four-year-old has just heard some wild stories about invisible snakes from older kids at school. He wants to get up to use the bathroom, but is afraid he will be bitten by an invisible snake.

Rather than saying, "That's stupid, there are no invisible snakes, just get up and do it," you can respond with more understanding.

DAD: "Johnny, why do you think there are invisible snakes under your bed?"

JOHNNY: "Joey told me about invisible snakes."

DAD: "How does Joey know about invisible snakes?"

JOHNNY: "He has them under his bed."

DAD: "Well, I don't know if he really does. If a snake bit him, he wouldn't have been around to tell you about them, would he?"

JOHNNY: "Maybe. But I'm afraid."

DAD: "That's okay. When I was little, I thought I had invisible snakes under my bed too."

JOHNNY: "Were you afraid?"

DAD: "At first. But sooner or later I got up and nothing happened. I thought maybe there weren't any snakes after all, or if there were, they were afraid of me. You got up last night and the night before and nothing happened, right?"

JOHNNY: "Yeah, I guess so."

DAD: "Take my hand and get up. You'll see that there aren't any invisible snakes, and if it turns out I'm wrong, I'll be here to protect you."

Slowly, Johnny takes your hand and gets up. He may be afraid at first, but when nothing happens he'll have just faced and overcome a fear.

The best thing is in years to come, you can even make this an analogy: "Is that a real fear or an invisible snake?"

When you tell your children about facing your fears and taking risks, and how taking risks has affected your life in a positive way, they will see themselves as emerging risk-takers who are following in well-trodden footsteps.

Chapter 9

Persistence

"Nothing in the world can take the place of persistence. Talent will not; nothing is more common than unsuccessful men with talent. Genius will not; unrewarded genius is almost a proverb. Education will not; the world is full of educated derelicts. Persistence and determination are omnipotent."

- Calvin Coolidge

"Fall seven times, stand up eight."
- Japanese Proverb

Persistence is a cornerstone of success. In fact, if there were to be one single element which would stand out from all other keys to success, it would be persistence.

The definition of persistence is "To set a goal and single-mindedly pursue that goal without giving up, regardless of the number of obstacles, setbacks, denials or failures, until that goal is attained."

There are countless examples of people who, because they refused to give up, went from nothing to extreme levels of success in all areas of life. Let's look at one well known example of persistence:

He was defeated for the legislature and lost his job in 1832.

His employer failed in 1833. The next year he failed in his own business. The same year he was elected to the legislature.

The year after that his girlfriend died.

In 1836 he had a nervous breakdown.

Two years later he was defeated in the election for Speaker of the House. He ran for Congress and lost in 1843.

He ran again in 1846 and won, then lost his re-election campaign in 1848.

The next year he tried to become a land officer and was not accepted.

He ran for Senate in 1854 and was beaten soundly.

In 1856 he was defeated in his attempt to become Vice President.

He ran for the Senate again in 1858, and lost again.

Finally, in 1860, he was elected President of the United States.

You know this man quite well. He was Abraham Lincoln, the man who abolished the single greatest crime against mankind in the history of the human race.

Another more example would be speed skater Dan Jansen, who won the Gold Medal in the 1994 Winter Olympics in the 1,000-meter race.

Before this Dan had been in three Olympics. Due to personal tragedies and just plain bad luck, he'd never won a medal.

Finally, in the last race of his Olympics career, he came in first place.

That's persistence!

Persistence is that "keep on keeping on" quality that defines the lowly ant, who never gives up, and the successful human being who reaches the highest pinnacle in his or her field.

As parents, we need to teach our children the value of persistence.

Children need to understand that persistence, combined with a good strategy, can help everyone reach all of their goals in life. They need to know its okay to fail, so long as they don't give up.

Two Qualities Your Children Need to Avoid

Two deadly qualities, which you need to teach your children to avoid at all costs, are the opposite of persistence. These qualities are complacency and procrastination.

Complacency is being satisfied with where you are or with what you've got.

At first, this might sound admirable. However, it is the enemy of forward motion in life.

For example a martial arts student has developed their endurance enough to run one mile. This doesn't mean that she shouldn't continue to develop her endurance until she can run three or even five miles.

Being satisfied or complacent at a performance level below your full potential is actually counterproductive. In order to live a fulfilling life you should strive to get the most out of it you can, as long as your life remains balanced.

Procrastination is, basically, inertia. It is the quality of putting off or stalling when things have to be done.

There are many reasons a person procrastinates: fear of failure, fear of change, fear of success. However, just as it takes initially greater effort to overcome the inertia of a rock at rest, once that rock is rolling, it's rolling. It doesn't change course it just keeps going.

Once your child begins a task, he must be taught to finish it, no matter how challenging it is.

Louis Pasteur said, "Let me tell you the secret that has led me to my goal. My strength lies solely in my tenacity."

After getting started, you must teach your children to persistently pursue goals until they are accomplished.

Although persistence is vital, it must be tempered with the ability to learn from mistakes.

"Perhaps there is no more important component of character than steadfast resolution," said Theodore Roosevelt. "The boy who is going to make a great man or is going to count in any way in afterlife must make up his mind not merely to overcome a thousand obstacles, but to win in spite of a thousand repulses and defeats."

To develop persistence, a child must first learn to accept that things don't always work out correctly the first time. Everyone learns from setbacks and failures.

It reminds me of a story about Mary and Ellen. They were 12-year-olds from the same city. They were close friends; however, Ellen was always slightly ahead of Mary.

While Mary's grades were acceptable; Ellen was at the top of the class.

However, Mary was a more naturally gifted athlete. She was bigger, stronger and faster.

Mary and Ellen had been training in martial arts for the same amount of time.

It was only natural that, when the school held an internal tournament, Mary soundly defeated Ellen in point (non-contact) sparring. Ellen congratulated her friend on her victory.

A few weeks went by and Mary took it as a given that she was much better at martial arts than Ellen. The instructor sensed this.

Mary's mother had also made him aware that she felt Mary was an underachiever in school. The instructor saw this as a chance to give Mary a valuable life lesson.

While practicing for an upcoming tournament, the instructor again paired Mary off with Ellen.

Mary objected. "That's really not fair," she whispered. "Everyone knows I can beat Ellen."

The instructor replied, "It's really not a good idea to just assume that you can 'take' this person or 'take' that person."

To which Mary answered, "But I've already beaten her."

The instructor nodded and the match began. Mary launched her lightning fast roundhouse kick but Ellen wasn't there. Ellen scored quickly and easily.

Every time Mary began an attack, Ellen easily defended. In the end, Ellen ended up scoring an impressive number of points. Mary walked away with zero.

After the match, the instructor explained, "Ellen didn't look upon your win as her loss; she looked upon it as you teaching her that she had something to learn. You had better moves, and she studied them. This time, she was ready for your moves, so she won."

Mary took the words to heart. She didn't look upon her loss to Ellen as a defeat; she looked upon it as a lesson.

She had been so confident after her victory; she hadn't worked hard to improve her skills. After learning that this was a mistake, she applied herself with greater dedication.

Soon, this dedication filtered down to her schoolwork and her grades began to improve. At the end of the year, two students were tied for first in the class: Mary and Ellen.

Everyone learns from setbacks and failures. Persistence without learning can turn into mere frustration. Persistence aligned with learning turns into rapid accomplishment of goals.

Persistence Starts with a Goal in Mind

"Start with the end in mind."
- Stephen Covey

To accomplish anything, it must be something we've decided to do in advance.

A goal is something that we have decided to accomplish, and are willing to work for. It's that pure and simple.

We owe it to our children to help them learn to set goals as early as possible in life, perhaps as early as three or four years old. Of course, at that age those goals are going to be small and short term, but this begins to develop the qualities of a goal-oriented person.

As your child becomes older, you can help him/her set bigger, more long-term goals, all the while allowing for the developmental stage of the child.

How Can You Help Your Child Set and Achieve Goals?

First, you must set a good example. You have to be a goal setter and achiever.

We'll go back to this point over and over in this book, so much so that we'd like you to burn it into your mind right now, before we proceed:

"You can't teach what you don't know!"

If you yourself aren't setting goals right now, get started.

The goal-setting procedure we'll outline for your children will also work for you. In the chapter on goal setting we'll even help you and your child more specifically.

In a nutshell, goal-setting is a five-step process:

1) Decide what needs to be done.

2) Decide what action is needed to accomplish this.

3) Perform this action.

4) Check your results to see if you've achieved your goal.

5) Go back to step one.

A very good device for setting goals is to use the S.M.A.R.T. method. S.M.A.R.T. is an acronym for Specific Motivational Attainable Relevant and Trackable.

Let's say your child's goal is to be accepted at a certain college. Using the S.M.A.R.T. method, his first task would be to be Specific, which would be to write down "I will be accepted at Blank University."

Notice the specific language. Not "I want to be accepted," but "I will be accepted."

For a goal to be real your child must visualize themselves accomplishing their goal in advance to successfully complete it. They cannot simply want it.

Next, make the goal Motivational to your child.

In this case, the motivation is obviously being able to enter the career of choice. No matter the reason, there has to be a motivating factor. And, additionally (especially on the subject of college), it has to be your child's goal, not your goal, not the peer group's goal, nor anyone else's.

Third, your child's goal needs to be Attainable. When you help your child set a goal, make sure it's something within the realm of possibility.

If, for example, the goal is to play on the soccer team, she needs to have a good idea of what it takes to get on the team and be willing to put in the time and effort to attain it. The goal must be within reach.

Children should have high aspirations, but they also need to learn about acceptable limits. If your child is four-feet eleven inches tall and 90 pounds and wants to be a forward for a professional basketball team, it's time to reassess their goal.

The next part of this method is doing things Relevant to attaining the goal.

For example, if their goal is to be a black belt in the martial arts in three years and she practices martial arts once a month and practices volleyball three times a week, she'll become a good volleyball player, but not a black belt.

That's because her energy is devoted to something not Relevant to her stated goal. To achieve goals, our primary focus of energy must be on things that help achieve that particular goal.

The final part of our acronym is that the goals are Trackable.

Almost every goal can be subdivided; that is, broken into smaller parts or mini-goals. If your child's goal is to get into a certain college, she must first set a mini-goal of determining that college's admission requirements, then set additional mini-goals of achieving those requirements, such as maintaining a certain grade level, taking certain courses, etc. It's called strategy.

Quite often, in attaining certain goals, the strategy must be adjusted and fine-tuned as one goes along, just as a pilot sets a course, but must make many minor alterations in the course to adjust for wind, timing, and so on.

By having trackable goals, it makes it easier to attain the final goal. This is because the energy is devoted to specific segments, not diluted out over a major undertaking. Tracking a goal also makes it easier to see when one is off course.

Now that you've learned how to help your child develop goals, let's look at various ways to help your child develop persistence through goal setting.

Using Goals to Teach Persistence

"Many of life's failures are people who did not realize how close they were to success when they gave up."

- Thomas Edison

Persistence requires believing in yourself and in your ability to overcome adversity. Since life is full of adversity, understanding how to work through problems is an important aspect of having a successful life.

To teach persistence you need to help your children believe in their ability to overcome the problems they encounter. By "problems" I don't mean something negative. In fact, we can change our meaning slightly and improve our perception of "problems" by changing the label to "challenges."

Helping set goals can be done through asking questions of your child. So can teaching persistence.

Let's say your child wants to improve her grade in spelling this year by 10% or by one grade level. Let's imagine that this would be an improvement from 70% to 80% or from "C" to "B."

The first thing you need to do is to point out to her that this is a goal. You might say, "Well, that's your goal. Let's write down 'I will get a 'B' in spelling this year'."

Now, you're probably asking two questions. The first might be "Why settle for just a 'B' when the child should be getting an 'A'."

Again, if you've evaluated your child (not in your wishes or expectations, but reality) as capable of getting an 'A,' and feel a 'B' is complacency, you have a talk with your child about reevaluating and resetting the goal.

But if your child's goal is realistic, you give your child your support.

Next question: "Why write it down?"

By writing her goal down your child has made commitment to it. She has put herself on record as wanting to achieve that goal.

Her commitment improves the chance of her continuing to follow through on the goal. Additionally, it makes it easy to see the smaller parts, or subsets (mini-goals) the larger goal needs to be broken into.

It's goes back to the old question, "How do you eat an elephant?"

The answer is "One bite at a time!"

By learning to set mini-goals your child is learning a way to correct her course when necessary.

Now that you've helped your child decide on what her goal is and have helped her break it into smaller parts, it's time to write down the plan.

For example:

Challenge: Getting a "B" in spelling.

Strategy: This year I will get a "B" in spelling. This is how:

1. I will study spelling 15 minutes every morning when I wake up and 15 minutes at night before I go to bed.

2. I will focus on breaking the words into phonics and changing those phonics into spelling parts.

3. I will have mom or dad quiz me on the spelling words the night before a spelling test.

4. I will write out the words I get wrong on this quiz ten times each.

5. If I don't find myself improving, I will increase my study time and ask the teacher for pointers.

6. If I find myself improving beyond my expectations, I will reset my goal to get an "A" in spelling.

These steps outline what the child wants and how she intends to go about getting it. It also tells her how to correct the course and evaluate (while tracking) the goal.

Now let's look at teaching persistence.

For the first four weeks, your child is getting "A's" in spelling. Then, as children sometimes do, she starts to feel she's achieved her goal, and slacks off.

The fifth week she comes home with a "C."

What you don't want to do is go into an "I told you so!" or "I knew you wouldn't stick to it" mode. Instead, you take this opportunity to help her persevere in her goal.

The conversation might go something like:

"Dad, I got a 'C' on my spelling test."

"How do you feel about that?"

You're asking a question to find out how well she remembered how excited she was when she first planned the goal, and then how she felt when she started to see fruit from her labors.

"Not very good."

"What are you going to do about it?"

"I'm not sure, Dad."

"Well, let's take a look at your goal sheet and see if that can help us."

Of course, when you look at the goal sheet there is specific language on how to improve spelling grades. It's in her own writing, and she sees what she needs to do to improve. This helps to put her back on course.

How Goal Setting Improves Persistence

Taking the time to set a goal and put it on paper helped her remember that she had committed to making a better grade. It also reminded her that she knew how to achieve it.

Although she had a bad week, it wasn't her whole grade. Using her goal sheet, she could readjust her course and still get the grade she had set for her goal.

Without the written-down goal, once the excitement of the new goal had died and the first low grade came in, your child would probably do what most people do and say, "Oh, well, it seemed like a good idea at the time."

She would basically be saying to herself "I'm just a 'C' student."

This would be giving up at merely the first obstacle! By having her goal written down, she can review what she had set for herself.

Additionally, this review can recapture the mood she had when she first wrote the goal down and re-stimulate her enthusiasm. She will also review the part where she wrote down her "back-up" plan if her initial plans didn't seem to be working.

By reviewing her own words written in her own writing, she is ten times more empowered toward working toward her goal than she would be by anything you could say verbally! By having set her goal herself and looking back on it, she is also learning responsibility.

As a result, she becomes more action oriented and more willing to try things she may not do well in the beginning. This improves her self-esteem and her desire to set and achieve other meaningful goals in the future.

Help Your Child See Setbacks as Learning Experiences

"Every mistake is an opportunity for learning."
- Ralph Waldo Emerson

One thing we can be sure of: life will give us plenty of setbacks. The longer we live, the more goals we set, and the higher these goals become. Therefore, we're going to encounter a greater number of setbacks and detours.

What you don't want to do for your children is to teach them to rate themselves as successes or failures through their goals.

You do want your children to become conditioned to take failure as a challenge, spurring their determination and perseverance.

> *"Our greatest glory is not in never falling, but in rising every time we fall."*
>
> **- Confucius**

Success is a result of Effort

To help your children see failure as a challenge you need to support them and help them see themselves as successes for trying their best.

Now this is not to say that we reward mediocre performance, far from it. We are advocating rewarding the best performance your child can truthfully give.

If your child is playing baseball and he strikes out all three times, when you drive him home he's going to be feeling pretty down.

Don't tell him not to worry about it. This is simply not good feedback because it won't motivate him to improve.

Instead, point out something specific that he did well, like "Well, you did a pretty awesome job in the outfield. You caught that fly, and you got the ball to Billy in time to let him tag the other player out at first.

And you know, tomorrow's Sunday. We'll practice your batting for a couple of hours. Feel like pizza?"

The Spider's Lesson

Persistence is the one ingredient that truly separates those at the top from the also-rans and wannabes. From George Washington to Ronald Reagan, from Edison to Einstein, persistence is the one lesson that can be found in the biographies of literally anyone who ever made it big.

The original demonstration of this quality is credited to a Scottish Warrior named Robert the Bruce, or, more originally, to a spider whose acquaintance he made.

Having fled from the might of the oncoming armies before the battle of Bannockburn, he was hiding in a cave, tired, defeated and depressed. He had failed, things had not gone as planned, and the future looked hopeless.

Many of us have been to our own "cave" at various times in our lives. Any fool can get up and have a great day when things are going great. It's when things are not so good that the real winners and losers in life are truly decided.

After sleeping for several hours, he woke up to see a spider had spun a huge web that almost reached across the entire mouth of the cave. Before the spider could complete its task, a strong gust of wind blew the web to pieces.

Undeterred, the spider climbed back to the top of the cave and started spinning the web again. Three times the wind howled through the cave and destroyed the web. Yet each time, the spider climbed back to the top and started spinning the web all over again.

Robert watched this spider for hours as it spun its web, and he searched his very soul for answers to overcome the seemingly insurmountable strength of his enemy. Then, from this simple scene, Robert the Bruce saw the answer so clearly and simply that he drew from it immense strength and purpose.

The following day, he rounded up his weary men and led them back into battle. They defeated the enemy despite being vastly outnumbered. The spider's message rings out today just as loudly and clearly as it did hundreds of years ago:

"If at first you don't succeed, try, try again!"

Chapter 10

Attitude

"Once upon a time there was a man who was walking through the woods. Suddenly a huge tiger jumped out and started chasing him.

He ran from the tiger to the edge of the path and found that the path ended at the side of a cliff. The tiger was closing in on him, so he lost his balance and slipped.

As luck would have it, a strawberry vine was sticking out of the side of the cliff, and he grabbed it and held on. Slowly, the vine began to pull out from the side of the cliff.

The man looked up and saw the tiger, flashing sharp white teeth at him. He looked down at the sharp rocks hundreds of feet below. Then he looked at the vine, slowly pulling out of the cliff, an inch at a time, and saw one lone strawberry growing.

So he picked it and he ate it, and he said to himself, "This is the best strawberry I've ever tasted."

- Chinese parable

Attitude is kind of an elusive term. It can be defined as one's opinion or outlook, the stance which one takes, but it is more of a term which must be felt than defined.

It means a little more than the definition.

Attitude is one's opinion, outlook and stance toward a specific subject, to be sure, but it is more instinctive and more the result of conditioning than a simple evaluation of the facts as one sees them. As a result, it's more difficult to change.

While an opinion can be changed simply by presenting additional facts, an attitude is more inherent and therefore more difficult to change.

An attitude is more of a feeling than a thought.

Negative Attitude

For example, a person who drives in a congested, metropolitan area is subject to a massive bombardment of negative feelings about other drivers. Drivers compete for parking places, they speed, they tailgate, they behave rudely. When a driver is courteous, it goes unnoticed as the courteous driver isn't a threat to life, the rude driver is.

Ultimately the individual develops a very negative attitude toward other motorists. He presumes that the other driver is going to do something wrong before the other driver gets a chance.

Nearly every motorist has had two experiences. The first is that the motorist sees another driver who appears to be having difficulty entering the lane of traffic. The motorist is courteous, slows down, and allows him to enter.

The driver who was allowed to enter then proceeds to drive at an extremely slow speed, ignoring all of the motorists behind him and obstructing traffic. The courteous driver feels "No good deed goes unpunished," and vows to never again let someone in front of him.

The second experience is when the motorist attempts to enter traffic. There is plenty of room to make a safe lane change, but the driver in the next lane speeds up and cuts him off, so he can't enter.

The motorist in the second example was either very immature ("me first!") or assumed that the driver would behave like the driver in the first example, and wasn't about to take a chance.

In other words, the motorist in the second example had a negative attitude toward other drivers.

The point of these examples is to demonstrate through everyday occurrences that there is one vital difference between opinion and attitude: attitudes are not assumed, they are developed. Once a person has developed an attitude, it is very hard to change.

Sadly, we live in times where bad attitudes are the norm. When we go shopping, are we greeted by courteous and enthusiastic sales clerks, or do we have to do battle with the store's employees simply to purchase a product? A friend recently went shopping at a large computer megastore, and sarcastically wrote, after several experiences trying to purchase product:

"I think this is the store's training manual:

1. Avoid customers at all times.

2. When you have to pass customers, aggressively avoid eye contact.

3. When the customer tries to force eye contact, speed up to look like you're in a hurry to help someone else.

4. Never be in your own department. That way, when a customer steps in front of you to stop you, you can say, "I don't know. You'll have to ask someone who works in this department."

Of course, if the system works as played, they'll be in some other department.

In short, today's workers have developed an attitude that the customer is the enemy. This is a byproduct of modern living.

Due to the absorption of smaller stores by megastores, the large chain stores keep prices competitive by keeping a minimal sales staff and providing marginal training. It can also be taken as a certainty that the sales staff is not well compensated.

Again, the sales clerk develops an attitude, "I can work hard for minimum wage or I can goof off for minimum wage. Sounds like a no-brainer to me."

These are examples of negative attitude.

The reason we are dwelling on negative attitude at the beginning of this chapter is because positive attitude is not the opposite of negative attitude. Positive attitude and negative attitudes are two sole and separate frames of mind. Therefore, it is possible to have both positive and negative attitudes at the same time.

An example of this mind-set is a businessman who is weaving in and out of traffic. Each time the light turns yellow, he speeds his Mercedes through the light, nearly killing innocent motorists (or even pedestrians!) in the process.

When a driver gets in front of him driving at a safe (not excessively slow) speed, he mouths bitter vulgarities.

The reason? n his mind he's stating, "I'm on my way to close the biggest deal of my life, I'm going to close that deal, and nobody's going to get in my way!"

An example of both positive and negative attitudes.

Negative Attitude is Learned Behavior

Since it is possible to have both a positive and negative attitude at the same time, before we go into the importance of developing a positive attitude, let's examine the ways in which you can prevent your child from developing a negative attitude.

A child develops a negative attitude either directly or indirectly. A directly developed negative attitude is a response to actions done directly to the child.

An example of this could be a child who is the victim of abuse at the hands of another child or the schoolyard bully.

Say Sally is very fond of playing with Polly. The only problem is that Polly is a hitter. From time to time, Polly will take a swing at Sally and strike her, causing her pain.

If this continues, Sally will develop a negative attitude toward others, feeling others will cause you pain at any given time. This must be nipped in the bud.

Adult intervention during the primary years is a tricky thing. It can lead to belittling of the child ("Tattle-tale!") or even retribution from the child doing the bullying. It can also reinforce in the child's mind that she cannot resolve problems with others on her own. She must seek outside help.

Before I go to any length with advice, I'm going to caution the reader. I do not believe in violence, and I do not believe in fighting. On the other hand I do believe, very much, in self-defense.

The best course of action would be to instruct Sally to tell Polly that she doesn't like being hit. Sally should talk about it to Polly.

She needs to tell her that it hurts and ask her to please not do it again. If this doesn't work, it's time for more drastic measures.

Sally needs to tell Polly, "I like playing with you. You're my friend. I like you. But if you hit me again, I will hit you back two times harder." And, if it happens again, Sally must then hit back two times harder.

Again, I am not advocating a fight. What I am advocating is letting Polly know how it feels.

Of course, much of this depends on the situation. If Polly is a little sadist who enjoys inflicting pain on others, Sally will have to find a new friend.

If the solution doesn't work, Polly must be barred from Sally's life. But if Polly is banished before Sally is allowed to try to resolve the situation on her own, Sally will feel as if she has failed (and lost a friend).

Allowing her to take direct action and attempt to resolve the situation personally gives a lot better chance that Sally will not develop a negative attitude.

Another example is suppose Chris complains to you, his parent that Billy cheats on his tests. Chris has been taught integrity, and finds this wrong, but he is disturbed because Billy got an A by cheating and Chris got a B following the rules.

It is important to encourage Chris with words like, "Billy got an A by breaking the rules. You got a B without cheating. Billy's A is a lie. Your B is real. Isn't someone who can get a B by playing fair smarter than someone who has to cheat to get an A?"

This will go a long way to quell Chris' anger, and prevent him from developing a negative attitude.

By far, most negative attitudes are learned indirectly. As with most things with children, it is learned from the parent.

Usually, negative attitudes are encouraged by parents through the serious mistake of comparison.

If a parent makes a statement like, "Mrs. Jones was bragging again about how Jimmy gets all A's and here you are a C student." This will make the child very resentful of Jimmy.

This can also happen internally in a family with statements like "Why can't you be more like your brother?"

Statements like this encourage the wrong kind of competitive spirit. They can make a child feel inferior, and develop a negative attitude toward others.

Resentment is like a weed that grows larger as a person gets older. A person who grows up being compared to others or having the superior performance of others pointed out looks upon other people as the competition, always out to get "one up" on him. This person can develop a terribly negative attitude about other people.

Negative attitudes can also be learned by imitating the parent. Most readers are sure to have had this experience: You pull up to a restaurant with your family to enjoy dinner on a Friday night. Another family arrives at just the same time. The other family sees you, and immediately speeds up their pace to get through the door before you.

Sometimes a parent will even yell, "Come on!" or "Hurry up!" at the child so that they can achieve the all-important goal of getting in through the door first.

These children are being taught to harbor a very negative attitude. They are learning that others get in the way and are to be competed with. Other people are viewed as "the enemy."

This can be seen every day, from the shopper who speeds up to get in the supermarket line before another shopper (often with a child accompanying him/her) to the mother who grabs both of her children when another concession line is opening up in a movie theater, and physically pushes them so they'll be first in line.

People who are nurtured this way develop the attitude that all other people are "the competition." By the very nature of the term, competition exists to be defeated.

A much healthier attitude to implant in a child would be one of, "We don't have to be in such a hurry," or "Why rush? Enjoy the walk."

If your child points out the other family hurrying to get ahead, you should point out, "It's really not that important to get through the door first. Maybe they're in a hurry, but we don't have to be."

This goes the same for pointing out the behaviors you don't want your child to adopt, for example, smoking. The key is to point of the behavior in a way that does not attack the person who is smoking, while still allowing your child see smoking for what it is.

A fact of life is that there will come a time when your child will be tempted to smoke cigarettes. They're easy to get, and children view smoking as something adults can do as they can't; therefore, smoking a cigarette is an entrance into the adult world.

When you pass a child or teenager smoking and you're with your own child, it's important not to say something like, "Look at that dumb kid smoking."

Your child will hear the operative word, "kid." He will interpret this as, "Dad thinks he's dumb because he's not supposed to smoke because he's a kid." In other words, it will reinforce in his mind that smoking is an adult thing.

It would be far more effective to make a remark like, "Look at him smoking. I wonder if he realizes how young that makes him look."

Most children try smoking to appear or to feel older. If you reinforce the idea that a child smoking looks younger (because he has to make an effort to look older), your child will view smoking as childish.

A side note is that this is a little more ticklish if you smoke yourself. It can have the overtones of hypocrisy.

However, you can turn a negative into a positive with a confession like, "Tommy, when I was your age, I wanted to look older. I thought smoking would make me seem older because the grown-ups were doing it. But cigarettes are very habit forming and they can damage your health. And once I started, I couldn't stop. It really didn't make me feel any older, it actually made me look younger, and now I'm hooked. I don't want that to happen to you." (It also might be the kick in the pants you need to quit.)

Aggressive driving is another area where a little "criticizing without criticizing" can go a long way.

If for example, you and your older child see a newly licensed 16-year-old driver speeding or squealing his tires, a comment like, "What an idiot!" can make a child think, "Dad's just jealous because Morty's so cool!"

On the other hand, a remark like, "He doesn't feel very good about himself so he squeals his tires to get attention" is a lot more effective.

Remember, negative attitudes, once they become part of the psyche, are very difficult to erase. It's better to arm your child with a lack of these negatives before they ever begin to develop.

Positive Attitude

As we stated previously, a positive attitude is not the opposite of a negative attitude. Both of these attitudes can exist simultaneously in one mind. It is easier, however, to develop a positive attitude than it is to erase a negative one.

First, let's deal with what a positive attitude is not. It is not denial, it is not self- brainwashing, and it is not the "ostrich approach," where one buries one's head in the sand and hopes that, by ignoring negative possibilities, they won't go away.

There has been much said about the so-called "power of positive thinking," where one only holds the positives in one's mind with the projected outcome being, therefore, positive. The danger with this mind-set is that there are such things as human limitations and random whims of fate ("bad luck"), and if one doesn't consider the possibility of a negative outcome, one isn't prepared for it.

The idea behind a positive attitude relates to the example of the race driver in our chapter on Focus.

The race driver, driving at a tremendously high speed, knows that the car will instantly go where his attention is focused. He focuses on the gap between the car beside him and the wall and the car goes through this gap. The reason he focuses on this gap is because he's all too aware of the negative possibility of becoming a decoration on the wall if he loses his focus.

The person with a positive attitude, therefore, is aware of all of the possibilities in a given situation, including the possibility of a negative outcome. However, with all of these possibilities in mind, he or she focuses on the positive. The intent is to affect a positive outcome with this focus.

This is not to say that some sort of "magic" will kick in and deliver the desired outcome. It still takes work to achieve an outcome. The person with the positive focus concerns themselves with the ultimate result.

He or she is aware that it may take several tries, and there may be several failures along the way. However, if the focus is positive, the intention is that, if failure results, the person with the positive focus will continue to try.

A child with a positive attitude is generally well-liked, and seems to radiate a certain charisma. The reason for this is because people like people around whom they feel comfortable, and a person who's always looking at the bright side, as opposed to a person who's always complaining, makes others feel comfortable.

An example of a positive attitude can be had by contrasting two people in similar situations.

Joe is on his way to a business meeting. His tire blows out. Cursing his fate, he gets out and changes the tire. He arrives at the meeting late and is very surly.

The others are unimpressed, he doesn't get his point across, and no one really likes him. He leaves thinking, "If not for that tire blowing out, things would have gone my way!"

Jack is also on his way to a meeting when his tire blows out. Immediately, he goes to a nearby restaurant and calls ahead, letting them know what happened and that he will be late.

He then goes back to his car and changes the tire. During the time he is doing this, he goes over his speech in his head and edits it, refining his presentation.

He goes back to the restaurant and washes up and arrives an hour late. He begins with a brief joke about the situation, and then goes into his presentation.

He is very successful. The people attending the meeting are ready to cut him slack because they've all been in that situation, and he made positive use of the time it took to change the tire.

He leaves thinking, "Wow. It's a good thing that tire blew out!"

A positive attitude is basically the old "Is this glass half-full or half-empty?" question. It's a way of looking at things. For example, if something isn't working right, a positive attitude doesn't look at that thing as "broken"; a positive attitude looks at it as something that needs to be fixed.

It's relatively easy to raise a child with a positive attitude if you, the parent, are capable of pointing out the bright side of every situation. If your child comes home depressed over a bad grade on a test, the worst thing you can do is scold him for not working hard enough.

It's far better to make this lemon into lemonade by saying something like, "Well, Johnny, you know what grades are for. They're not to tell us if you're good or bad, or dumb or smart, they're to help us figure out the areas where you need work. Yes, you didn't get the best grade, but now we know where you have to concentrate in your studies."

Again, in school, it must always be stressed that a bad grade isn't to point out where a student is deficient; it's to point out what the student needs to work on in order to improve.

A child must also be helped in shaping his or her attitude toward people. If Joey comes home and says something like, "Stevie's fat!" you can probably find something good about Stevie to point out to your child.

It's easy to point out the positive: "Now, remember when you were sick and Stevie brought you those comic books?" or, "Well, he's also very good-natured and nice. And he's always telling those funny jokes."

Creating a Lifetime Positive Attitude

The perfect device for raising a child with a positive attitude is to always counter complaints with this simple request: "Okay, I understand that, and I agree that that's bad. Now, tell me something good that happened today."

Your child may think and immediately come up with something good, or it may take a little help.

You might ask, "Did you play soccer this afternoon? Did your team win? Great!"

If the team didn't win, you can say something like, "How many points did you score? Well, that's nothing to be ashamed of!"

By getting your child to immediately counter negative feelings by listing the positive things that happened in a day, you will get him/her into the habit of deliberately trying to find the good.

Sometimes, situations arise that are simply bad situations. It's not always possible to make lemonade out a lemon. What if the lemon is dry or rotten?

In this case, the idea is not to venture into the realm of denial or cockeyed optimism with a silly statement like, "Well, your bike was stolen, yes, but at least it was parked and they didn't beat you up and take it."

Sure, this didn't happen, but it can always be worse but this will not ease the pain of losing the bike, or negate the fact that the bike is now gone.

The thing to do in a situation where there is no positive outlook is to venture in the only positive direction there is for such situations: they are learning experiences.

If you say "Okay, I'm sorry your bike is gone. But tell me, what did you learn from this?" your child may think for a long time, and come back with a response like, "To be more careful with my things. I should have locked it."

If he doesn't come up with a response like this, you may have to help him with a statement like, "Did you lock it?" If he says "No," don't scold him with an angry, "Why not! Do you know how much I paid for that bike? How careless of you!"

While that may make you feel better you need to remember he's just a kid. He's feeling punished enough by the consequence of the loss of his bike.

Instead, a response like, "So what did you learn?" will go a much greater distance toward creating a positive attitude. Your child will have learned to be more careful with his possessions, and a growth experience will have taken place.

Writing Down Positives

The final step toward creating a positive mind-set is to have your child write down the good things that happened. Again, if, every night, he or she is required to write down and list at least three good things that happened during the day, he or she will get into the habit of looking for them.

This will get your child into the habit of focusing on positive things which will help your child develop a positive mindset.

If something bad happens, the same technique can be used. A child can write down the series of events like a formula:

What happened?

What did I learn?

What was the result?

For example:

"My bike was stolen."

"I have to be more careful."

"I'll keep an eye on my things."

Another example:

"I got a C in math."

"I need more work in math."

"I'll study my math harder."

Once you have gotten your child into the habit of looking for the positive, you will have armed your child, with a lifetime of positive focus.

Chapter 11

Character

Stop me if you've heard this one before:

A turtle was sunning itself on the beach. A scorpion walked up and said, "Will you give me a ride to the island?"

The turtle said, "No way. You'll sting me."

The scorpion said, "No, I promise not to sting."

The turtle was reluctant, but the scorpion pleaded and begged. Finally, the turtle gave in and let the scorpion climb on his shell.

He swam out to the island and climbed onto the shore. Just as the scorpion was getting off of his back, the turtle felt the scorpion's stinger sink into his neck.

Everything started getting blurry. As the turtle began to black out it said, "You promised that if I helped you that you wouldn't sting me."

The scorpion said, "I know, and I really tried. But it's my nature to sting."

- parable of unknown origin

Now, when one hears this parable, the question is "Am I a scorpion or a turtle?"

Most people will mull this over. But if you are honest, the response will be, "I'm a little of both".

It's not that you don't have both inside of you but rather how much, or the degree, of scorpion or turtle a person is that determines their character.

Scanning the Yellow Pages, when martial arts studios are advertising classes for children and teens, one frequently sees the slogan "Build character!"

Yet, when one asks the average person, "What is character?" quite often the person asking the question receives a very puzzled look. Usually, the response is something like, "Being a good person."

What exactly is meant by the term "character"? Now, we're not talking about a person in a movie, like the good guy or the bad guy, we're talking about the personality trait of character. What it really means is a person's nature.

All human beings follow their basic nature. Character is an inherent personality trait. Most people are either of superior or inferior character.

It would be too simple to state that this means people are either good or bad. Most people have both good and bad traits, and if there are more good traits than bad we deem that individual to be a good person, if there are more bad traits than good, we assume the reverse.

It is important that we make our value judgments of a person's character based on that person's overall behavior, not on specific, isolated incidents. Every human being has failings.

Sometimes very bad people are capable of doing very good things, and very good people are capable of doing very bad things. It depends on circumstances.

If a person has a general tendency to try to do good, we can say he is of good character, and if a person has a general tendency to do things of a bad nature, we can assume he is of inferior character.

A person of good character is a person who, given several options, will take what we call the "high road."

For example, say a student wants to get an "A" on a test. A student of good character will learn the material, possibly ask a parent or teacher for help studying, and give it a best effort.

On the other hand, a student of bad character will tend more to try to get a copy of the exam, use cheat notes, etc. We might say he takes the "low road."

How to Assess Character

If we really don't know a person well, how do we tell if he or she is of good or bad character?

First, as a general rule, water seeks its own level. There is an old Spanish saying which, translated into English means: "Tell me who your friends are and I'll tell you who you are."

This implies that if a person is more comfortable around people of low character, we can assume he is of low character.

This is not to say that a good person can't have bad people around her; sometimes through business dealings or just random circumstances, a person may find herself around people of questionable character. But if she is of good character she will be very uncomfortable around them.

On the other hand, if a person always seems to seek out and bond with people of bad character, then we can assume that person isn't really worth knowing.

Building Character

What are some of the "red flags" concerning character?

Native Americans believed that our own worst qualities are the things that annoy us the most about others. In other words, if a person is always worrying about people stealing from him, to the point of being irrational about it, chances are that person will steal anything that isn't nailed down. If a person seems to be paranoid of other people, feeling they were trying to get the advantage in some venture, chances are that person is always trying to take advantage themselves.

Does this mean we have to live in shells, fearful of constantly being stung by scorpions? Does this mean we have to carefully scrutinize everybody for "red flags" of bad character?

Of course not! And it certainly doesn't mean we have to become judgmental and point at people and say, "Good character," "Bad character!"

It just means that, as a general rule, we should be aware of the overall conduct of people around us. That, under certain circumstances, we observe whether they tend to take the "high road" of integrity, honesty, and consideration of others, or "low road" of dishonesty, lack of principles, and "me first!"

The saying "Love is blind" was never more true when it comes to parenting. Often, teachers complain that a student will be caught red-handed doing something wrong, and a parent will come to school and confront the teacher.

"My child says he didn't do it," the parent insists, "and my child doesn't lie."

Just as we can evaluate our own character by looking at the things that make us angry about others, we can also evaluate our child's character the same way.

If, for example, little Suzy is always making statements like, "Mary's selfish. She never shares her candy," it's a good bet little Suzy isn't much into sharing herself.

A good approach might be to ask her, "Suzy, do you share with the other children?"

Now, of course, depending on the developmental stage, the response might be a lie, like "Of course I do!" when, in fact, she does not.

There's also the chance that Mary really might be stingy and Suzy might be generous, but you'll be able to determine the correctness of the response very quickly.

Once you've determined the reality of the situation, you can venture into an exercise in character building. It might be a good idea to give Suzy some candy, and suggest, "Here. This is for you to share with Mary. Then Mary will learn about sharing. Just offer her some of your candy, now. Don't say, 'I'm sharing with you, so next time you have candy, you have to share with me!' Just say, 'Mary, want some of this?' then we'll see what happens."

If Suzy does as instructed, several things will happen.

First, she will experience the joy of sharing with others. It sounds trite, but sharing something with other people generally does give a person, especially a child, a warm feeling.

Next, Mary will see that Suzy is a generous person. There will be some form of gratitude expressed, and Suzy, if she suffers from the trait of selfishness, will have made progress toward overcoming this trait and you will have a measurable result.

First, it must be impressed upon Suzy that sharing is a good thing, and she did not share with Mary as part of some manipulative testing ploy, to see if Mary would share with her. She shared with Mary merely for the sake of sharing.

What happens next is unpredictable. Perhaps Mary will immediately respond by bringing something to share with Suzy. Perhaps it will take a while.

Perhaps it will never happen, and perhaps Mary will again have candy and refuse to share it with Suzy. Each and every one of these outcomes can result in a character building opportunity.

If Mary does share with Suzy, the results speak for themselves. It's easy to point out: "You see! You shared with Mary, and now she's sharing with you. All it took was a little generosity on your part."

If Mary doesn't share, the old "Two wrongs don't make a right" example comes into play. "All right, maybe Mary is selfish, but you're not. Don't worry about Mary. Just be glad you're not that way. You can share."

Again, Suzy has been steered in the direction of superior character.

The Importance of Building Character at the Earliest Possible Age

When we use terms like "superior" and "inferior" in this context, we're not doing this to condemn others, or feel superior, we're doing this to help ourselves become better human beings. If our own worst behaviors are what annoy us the most about others, than we can let these feelings become a mirror of our own personalities and use what we learn to improve.

For example if a person says something to us that cuts us to the bone, maybe it's because we often say things to others that hurt them very deeply. This tells us that we should watch our tempers and our words and try to be more level-headed and kind with the things we say to others.

How many readers have had the experience of talking to another person about a third party?

The person you're talking to shakes his head and says, of the third party, "He's so negative!" Now ask yourself, isn't the speaker, the one calling another person "negative," usually one of the most negative people you know?

We can use this principle to evaluate and steer our children's character, as stated earlier in this chapter. However, it is important to note that character is an internal characteristic, and internal characteristics get locked in very early in life.

Many child psychologists believe that good and bad tendencies begin to develop in the preverbal years, and once these characteristics are locked in, they are very difficult to change.

If, for example, three-year-old Tommy is always hitting his little sister at home, he will probably become a hitter in school. It is important to find out why he feels it necessary to inflict pain on a defenseless individual, and impress upon him how wrong this is.

If he's always stealing his little brother's toys even though, as the older child, he probably has better toys, it's important to find out why and deal with it immediately.

The most common underlying reason for acting in the direction of inferior character is insecurity. A child, in fact any person who feels insecure takes the "low road" because he's not confident he can succeed on his own merit. If a child is behaving in a manner to indicate bad character, it's a strong probability that he, too, is acting out of insecurity.

How can three-year-old Tommy, who hits his sister or steals his brother's toys, be motivated by insecurity? Well, the reality is that he's acting out seeking parental attention and affection.

If Tommy is the oldest, until the arrival of his younger siblings, he was the center of his parents' universe. Then, suddenly younger children, who were helpless and requiring more attention, stole (in Tommy's perception) his parents' attention away.

In other words, he hits little sister out of retribution for taking something from him. He steals his little brother's toys because he believes that little brother has stolen from him (the affection of the parents).

Usually, the parents can correct this by altering their focus. Comments like, "Tommy, leave me alone! The baby's crying!" or "Tommy, let your sister have the balloon! She's younger than you!" only reinforce his attitude that something has been taken from him.

It's far better to start building his character by saying something like, "Tommy, your father and I love you very much. But now you have a little brother and a little sister, and you're going have to be a big brother to them. We need you to help us with them because you're the oldest."

This way, you're praising Tommy for being the oldest, and enlisting his help in raising the younger children. When they are babies, let Tommy hold them and help you bathe them and feed them. This way, he will look upon them as HIS younger brother and sister, not his rivals. Praise him when he does help.

If there is only one balloon and little sister is crying over it, say something more like, "Tommy, there's only one balloon and she's the little one. Don't you want your little sister to have it?"

Tommy is being asked to give something up, but in a positive manner and to HIS little sister. This way, he will be proud (hopefully) to give up the balloon to his little sister.

Of course, character building is an "iffy" proposition. We would be negligent if we didn't point out the fact that there will always be "incorrigibles." These are people who simply tend to go in the direction of evil for no apparent reason.

The basic nature of such children and, later, adults, is baffling and the sciences of evaluating such personality types are still in their infancy. Some attribute psychological factors such as childhood trauma. In the absence of these, some schools believe that there are biochemical imbalances; still others believe there are genetic traits, and so on and so on.

If you believe you are doing all the right things and your child's behavior still seems to be out of line, be sure to check with a mental health professional that works with children.

Confidence: The Cure for Insecurity

Under normal circumstances, barring personality disorders like someone who is a sociopath, the primary reason for inferior character, as stated, is insecurity. Kids don't usually do bad things because they are bad, they do them because they are insecure.

If an adult doesn't feel good about themselves they'll go outside of acceptable limits to succeed. They'll resort to sneaky plans and do shady things because they don't feel that they'll get ahead with their own talents or abilities.

They'll put others down because they feel inferior. They'll point out other people's deficiencies in order to draw attention away from their own deficiencies.

Once again, I'm going to invoke martial arts principles because martial art training is one of the few proven ways of overcoming insecurity. The confidence building aspect of martial arts is the character building aspect.

When you've proven yourself capable of failing and getting back up, trying again and winning, you gain self-confidence. When you see higher-ranking students doing things you can't do, and train, practice and find that you can, though your efforts, do these things, you realize that you can do just about anything you set your mind to.

And every time just one person realizes that he or she is worthy, and can succeed without breaking the rules or hurting another, that person takes a step on the road to building character. Each time just one person realizes that the things others do that hurt him or her are the same things he or she may be doing to others, that person will develop a different point of view.

And each time just one person starts to evolve into a person of character, the world becomes a slightly better place. We can't change the nature of others, but we can certainly change ourselves.

What I suggesting is the parent do the best possible job under the circumstances and to start early. If you follow the principles and do all within your grasp to always encourage your child to take the "high road," you will have done your best to "to arm your child with superior character.

Conclusion

All we have done is present data and offer advice. No two human beings are alike, and the methods for successfully empowering a child will vary from individual to individual.

We can only offer a time-tested strategy for empowering your child. It is up to you to fine-tune it as you go along. The ten attributes in this book are the weapons with which you can enable your child to face the world and come up a winner they were born to be.

As we move though this new millennium we can't predict what the world will be like ten or fifteen years from now. Hopefully, conditions will improve. But the fact remains that, for better or for worse, your child is going to be a part of that future. He or she will be a decision maker and hopefully a leader in that brave new world.

By following these concepts and interacting with your sons and daughters, you will go a long way toward preparing them to face that uncertain future.

You will have armed your child!

About The Author

Professor D's philosophy is that there is nothing more precious than physical and mental health. Because most of us are given these blessings at birth we often take them for granted. As a result we chase after fame and fortune and forget about those things that are most precious, that is until we begin to experience anxiety, a lack of sleep, poor health and even depression.

Professor D (Wil Dieck) began searching for ways of strengthen the mind and body when he began his studies of martial arts and human behavior over 4 decades ago.

As a long time martial artist and physical fitness fanatic, he studied martial arts in order to learn how to increase endurance, make the body stronger and become more flexible. Along the way he found that disciplines like Judo, Jujitsu, Tang Soo Do, Hapkido, Tai Chi, Qigong and Yoga could not only add to his physical health but also provided him with focus, calmness and mental stability.

His studies of psychology helped him gain insight into the workings of the human mind. He found that a person could actually learn to take back control of their mind through the use of technologies like Neuro Linguistic Programming and hypnotherapy as well as the discipline of Mindfulness Meditation.

Over the years he has passed on the information he's learned to his martial arts students as well as to the parents of his younger students (he continues to teach martial arts to children for the YMCA in San Diego.) He also regularly provides this information to students where he presently teaches, the University of Integrated Studies and ITT Technical Institute in San Diego, CA.

Professor D is the founder of Total Mind Therapy© and since 2006 has used it to help thousands of people create rapid, positive life transformations.

Professor D regularly gives talks to groups both large and small about how to maximize their potential and make the most of their lives. If you want more information about Professor D please visit the website http://www.BlackBeltMindSecrets.com/my_story or call (619)-293-3255.

Note: Wil Dieck began calling himself Professor D when many students in his college classes continually couldn't pronounce his last name correctly (it's pronounced DEEK) so he decided to make it easy for them all.